AF364992

The
Power
of the
Trumps
and Pips

CAMELIA ELIAS

The Power of the Trumps and Pips

OMNIBUS EDITION

The Power of the Trumps and Pips. Omnibus Edition © Camelia Elias. Published by EyeCorner Press 2020. DESIGNED AND TYPESET by Camelia Elias. IMAGES OF THE TAROT: Jean Noblet Marseille Tarot, 1650, as reconstructed by Jean-Claude Flornoy. By kind permission from Roxanne Flornoy.

ISBN: 978-87-92633-61-3
EBOOK ISBN: 978-87-92633-62-0

September 2020, Agger, Denmark

All rights reserved. No part of this book may be reproduced in any form, without written permission from the publisher and the copyright holder.

EYECORNERPRESS.COM

For Jean Grolier

Contents

THE BOOK IN FRONT OF YOU is an omnibus edition that gathers three types of texts: two previously published books, *The Power of the Trumps* (2017) and *The Power of the Pips* (2018), and unpublished lectures and essays. The motivation for this gathering is simple. As the texts stress the teaching of the Marseille Tarot by example, having a sustained focus on both the trump cards and the pip and court cards of the Marseille Tarot in one place is a good idea. Thank you to the readers who have wished for such an edition. You now get the 'power books' together in a form that highlights even more the usefulness of the Marseille Tarot, especially as the two books now appear here along with new method texts and other *inédit* material.

My other previous writings in book form on the Marseille Tarot had the function of succinctly introducing the reader to the method of reading these cards, in addition to delving into deconstructing traditional modes of interpretation. While *Marseille Tarot: Towards the Art of Reading* (2014) is an introduction book that also showcases the Carolus Zoya Marseille Tarot, unique in the world, *What is Not: Marseille Tarot à la Carte* (2019) uses a martial arts approach to reading visual texts, thus introducing the reader to the idea that seeing the obvious first, rather than going with archetypes and strange shadows, shallow empowerments, and clichés is infinitely more rewarding.

The idea with the omnibus edition here is to simply cut to the chase, as always, but make the cut a fuller one. For instance, the unpublished lecture presented here adds new and nuanced dimensions to the more traditional ideas regarding the symbolism and function of the pip cards. I look at how the pip cards embody connection, from creating coherence to burning bridges, and stress the notion that the pip cards are most useful when we see them as morphological and semantic markers. This material is original in the way it builds power around the function of the four suits. Thus, in addition to understanding what we do with cups, coins, batons, and swords, we look at concepts such as rulership and timing, the pips according to the alphabet, and situational, rather than symbolic calibrations. The examples draw on real life events, addressing topics such as perfectionism, procrastination, and pardoning.

As for the section on the trumps, the new here comes in the form of hammering on the idea that we stop limiting our reading skills by making recourse to symbolic associations. There's more to it than that. Considering the power of the function of the trumps over their symbolic and random accommodation is more dynamic and interesting, as the function of visually representing something opens the gate towards observing the subtle power of the obvious. As the obvious has a way of escaping us precisely because it's obvious, it is anchored in subtlety. In addition to what I already said initially in *The Power of the Trumps,* that here now also appears in a well-tempered hammering of seminal points, I stress the importance of improvising with the cards, rather than imitating existing cartomantic discourses.

The whole omnibus edition explores more keenly both the subtlety of the Tarot trumps and the pip and court cards configurations, demonstrating how this power translates into a concrete experience that can only be summed up like this: 'I'm reading the Tarot, and it feels like riding the hedge.'

The previously published books stand here together in a fresh relation of enhancement, strengthening each other's points. The new material consists of extending concretely the method of reading the Marseille cards to broadening the road towards understanding why considering the contextual before the investigative question is essential. The theoretical parts in this book cover formal design and its relation to systems of divination. The method part looks at the rationale behind our understanding of the use of the trump, court, and number cards, demonstrating how we can read them in a specifically situated context. Finally, the book is written in the vein of cultural criticism and philosophical deconstruction of language and the self, exemplifying life mirrored in 3 to 13 cards.

The present book is thus an exercise in applying the basic principles of interpreting the Marseille Tarot to the carefully forged and fitted context of current concerns, as they unfold against the background of investigations into chance and prediction, and reflection and evaluation, in other words, the domain of the fortuneteller. As with all my teaching and writing, at the heart of it is a simple invitation: think in a way that bursts open your perception. Don't think in terms of received perception. When the Tarot speaks to you, it doesn't speak in a language that's borrowed. It speaks in a language that you understand, as you cross the horizon line where the seen and the unseen mingle in an oracular, and poetic way.

*The Power
of the
Trumps*

Stumbling Into a Subtle Burst

T HE FIRST PART OF THIS BOOK features the trumps in the Marseille Tarot, as I initially presented them in a series of video lectures, where I talked about the power we can derive from the trumps both at the visual and methodical level. What you read here is basically the transcript of those lectures, enhanced. I like the idea of words following voice, as this is something I cover right here. I read sequences of three cards, just the trumps of the Marseille Tarot in this part, with a specific aim in mind. I intend to teach something about the power of the Tarot trumps, both at the individual and collective level. That is to say, I look at the cards as they appear next to one another, while also describing their force individually.

What interests me is power that's not so in your face, and therefore often stronger. This won't come as a surprise to occultists and animists, spiritual workers and other good folk who help people with their internal mess. For this group, power that manifests subtly is power that's interesting, power that's raw, dangerous, and not safe. While the whole of this book is another way of saying that you can learn what to do with the Marseille cards in terms of thinking of them as representations of embodiment, function, and voice, the book also gives you insight that runs at a subtler level, where what I explore is precisely this: a burst of power that's unmediated by culture. This is a tall order, as it's impossible to escape the symbolic mindset we all grow up with, and by 'symbolic mindset' I don't mean to suggest things like equating cups with love, but rather the mindset that tells us we're a success if we earn a lot of money, have a good education, an honest husband or wife, and obedient children. Now, doesn't all that make you soft in your knees? Of course it does, especially if you happen to be by the altar, saying yes, and buying the promise of everlasting happiness. Such is the work of belief: it's all symbolic, and we know it. It's all delusion, and we like it. But here's what I do here, other than laugh at our beliefs: I employ a simple method. I say something obvious. Then I ask you to think about it in different ways, and then I encourage you to stop thinking according to received perceptions.

Many talk about how the Tarot speaks to them. Indeed there is such a thing. Voice is the most magical tool we have, and it looks like inanimate objects also have it. But how concrete is what we hear? Putting what we hear into words, so that our understanding goes somewhere, is also an act of magic. What I do in this book that I haven't done in my other divination books is stress the bursting quality of the cards when it is experienced at the subtle level. By 'subtle' I mean the level that's in between articulations, on the surface of what moves, and then also just beneath it. We call this 'cultural context as mediated by images' in relation to what we sit with, the stuff in the heart, or the true question. This is less mysterious than it sounds. Just ask yourself: how many times have you sat with the images of the Tarot and had the feeling that although you see what you see, you also see more? I bet your answer to this is, 'many.'

Why do you think that is? Because subtlety has a voice. And this voice is more articulate than you think. It has a wider range than your whisper: 'Here be Dragons. I'm reading the Tarot and it feels like riding the hedge.'

So you start noticing the unseen that stares you in the face. The obvious is mysterious. It's mysterious because it's sharp and it has the face of the two worlds shape-shifting. You get a question about relationships, and off you go with reading embodiments, color, form, function, and fancy. How weird is that? It's weird because you take this job seriously, because you trust your feet firmly planted in two worlds. You're not riding this hedge because you want to act on dictations, cultural symbols and what's appropriate in their constructions. You're into other creations.

But what do you see? What *can* you see? Are you reading the Tarot with your full body, or are you transmitting consecrated thoughts, good ones, but sometimes uninspired because they are not yours? Where do you go, when you want to see what's what for yourself?

'I need to get there fast,' the Fool says. 'No time for walks here. I'll get in my car and teleport myself… Oops, it looks like I bumped into something. What was that?' Getting there fast, wherever it is you need to go to, is a great intention. But what if you forget something essential? Namely, that all Tarot readings are subject to conditions that change. What you point to right now when you look at a simple 3-card draw, can be contradicted by a fourth card. You may think: 'well, I was too eager. I brought this accident on myself.' But wait. Stop and look. What else is the Fool saying? 'Who's that other person falling out of the Tower?' 'What if it wasn't my fault?'

This is what happens when someone tricks you into taking the car, when you'd be better off walking, into taking him along as a clandestine passenger. This is someone who tells you: 'all this slow motion, you can do better. I'll give you directions.' Boom, the car hits a rock, or more rocks, the ones the Magician throws into the air that he pretends are his magic tools on his table. Before you know it, you're in for a ride, all right, but one that renders you in the ditch. So all is well until it's not anymore. You sigh. At least you can blame this on someone else. You can blame it on the fourth card showing up here, the con man.

If you ever get such card combinations that go from featuring single people on them to ones that feature several people on them, do you ever ask: who are these others? Do I know them? How do they impact on me? By way of force or inspiration? See, one of the guiding questions in all of my readings is in fact this very question: who is doing what to whom?

In my examples here, I offer a concrete contemplation on the problem of agency. I ask you to think about the power to act and who holds it. Is this power in the picture at all? The Tarot trumps are very clever at prompting us with this observation: how do we go from noticing who and what we're dealing with to the more refined, 'yes, but how does this impact on me, or the situation I'm in?' We have people cards, we have nature cards, and we have cards that tell us, 'you're also going to die.' Well, thank you cards.

It's good to know when a storm is coming, so I can call that a natural catastrophe if I see Judgment and the Tower together. One big cloud, and before you know it, everyone is directly affected. I don't need to speculate: 'who did this to me? Who are the others?'

The other question that interests me in this part of the book where I look at the subtle and bursting power of the trumps is the question of timing. Not so much timing in the sense of observing the dynamics between fast cards and slow cards — we've just had an example of that here, the Fool is slow, the Charioteer is fast — but more in the sense of when the time is right for something.

When you come to the cards with your question, you do so because the time is right for you to get answers that are more aligned with what your reality is and how it confronts you head on. After all, the only reason why you read cards is because you want to get away from culture and its discontents. You may know, culturally speaking, that it's a good idea to finish that education, stop bumming around and get in the fast lane. But what if the time is right for something else? What if you're done with working for an institution, and the time is right to walk away, do something else? You don't quite know what that is, because you're not trained to think outside of what culture dictates, but you know what you don't know that you *do know*. We call this logical intuition. So how do you see it in the cards *when the time is right for something?* This question of momentum is what I like to think of as the subtle burst in our readings, as it makes us go beyond symbolic power, beyond familiar patterns of thinking. This is the question that opens towards the possibility to read on target to utmost precision.

When the Tarot speaks to you, it doesn't speak in a language that's borrowed. It speaks in a language that you understand as you cross the line of what's appropriate. Come, ride on this hedge, and learn to think what not to think, learn to read the like the Devil, and get that penetrating vision going by reading the damn cards.

I Don't Know

WHY REGRET? people often ask me, whenever I read the card of the Hanged Man. Well, you see, traditionally, and by tradition I mean the evidence we find in old texts about the use of cards, the Hanged Man has been associated with treason. You betray your country, you'll find yourself hanged, and then drawn and quartered in the city square. This is a most gruesome practice of punishment, when the traitor would be tied to a wooden frame and then stretched beyond what the body's own flexibility would allow for. Sometimes being quartered simply meant being chopped up with an axe. This public act had one message only: 'it's regretful that some can't be loyal. The law punishes treason.'

As people would be witnessing the final breath of the tortured man or woman, they'd have their own regret, secret and unspoken of. This is a response appropriate for what culture wants: to instill fear. Culture doesn't like unusual, revolutionary ideas, because such ideas give you a taste for freedom. Freedom is culturally inappropriate because it can't be regulated, constricted, or contained. Freedom is bad news for culture, and society punishes bad news.

Most modern Tarot readers would go: 'you see things differently,' in their reading of the Hanged Man, and they'd be correct in their assumption. But...

What most fail to tell you is that seeing things differently can get you hanged, drawn and quartered, regretting your own actions, and ultimately having an ecstatic experience that you can't share with anyone because it's most certainly followed by death. Let us not forget that the trump following the Hanged Man is, after all, Death. But think of this Lover, Charioteer, and Hanged Man situation below:

So you say to yourself: 'I'm so going to make the right choice here. The blondie is the one for me. I like the wisdom of the brunette, she's older and more mature, but the blondie is better for my image.'

This is the Charioteer speaking, having the confidence of the young man, who, after some considerable vacillation and hesitation, is finally making his choice. Whatever internal conflict there may still be inside the heart, will be swept under the polished shining armor. What's an image good for, if you don't fling it to the public, flash it in all its virile construction?

But what if you betray something in your choice? What if the blonde woman is not the right one for you? What if your heart is somewhere else, in fact gone in the opposite direction, taking the path you didn't choose?

Ay, here comes the Hanged Man predicament. Regret. The grand standstill. Now what? Sometimes you bring this on yourself. Sometimes you're simply subject to external conditions. Sometimes you think you have just enough power to control your choices, but, as the image of the Lovers suggests, this is yet another grand illusion.

What do you suppose the presence of Cupid is there for? To inflame your passion, your love? Get real. Cupid is in the picture as a subtle, yet nasty reminder of the fact that you are never in control. You are always at the mercy of chance. If you're into prayers, then pray to Cupid that he shoots his arrow in such a way so that you experience the outcome as one of a perfect match: your heart in alignment with your conditions.

I don't get this common Tarot talk: 'follow your heart,' pertaining to the 'meaning' of the Lovers card. Yeah, right. Thank you very much. Can I now, please, also know what my heart wants? See, there's a reason why we talk about Mystery Traditions, most of them lost to the many. These initiatory methods of integrating your unconscious fears and desires with your conscious mind had a very good function: the function of saving you the trouble of regretting your choices, of imagining a number of 'what if' situations.

'What if I had picked the other one, the other man or woman, job, house, lover, and so on?' If you think you have time to speculate, then by all means. Suppose you realize all this while you're hanging. Suppose you realize that the little agency you have in the Lovers card, the flashing illusion of agency in the Charioteer's card is now completely gone, and you have one option only: to listen to the clock: tick, tock, tick, tock.

Suppose you're aware of the fact that there's a lot in between the tick and the tock of the clock. You become aware of the impressions that come to you, the tick, the tock, and other ones in between. Will someone save you, cut your rope, or not? Does it even matter? You're listening to the clock. That's where you're at. Whoa, that's pretty close to the mysterious, ecstatic experience. Suddenly the urge to 'keep going' has a deeper resonance for the Hanged Man than the one we associate with the Charioteer and his horses, or the Lover and his dames. Still, can he move, get himself out of what can't be helped?

Don't just think: 'I can follow my heart,' when you have no idea about what your heart wants.

Don't just think: 'I can control these horses,' when you have no idea about the nature of horses, or what comes next. What if a storm comes and topples your carriage? How confident will you be with your head in the ditch?

Don't just think: 'I'm having a new perspective,' when you're hanged. Who did this to you anyway? You don't even know.

Unless you're Odin or a skilled yogi who knows exactly what he's doing and why, you have no chance of surviving just because you have a different perspective, because you *know* things.

Put more succinctly, what is missing here is a clear sense of agency. Agency is presumed through will power, but is not really in the close-up picture. The Lover thinks he has it, though it's Cupid who has it. The Charioteer is convinced he has it, though the horses may have a different opinion. The Hanged Man hopes he has a whole lot of it, because, once transcended, he will be like God.

But to what extent are the Lovers, the Charioteer, and the Hanged Man aware of what they must give up in order for agency to occur?

If we look closely, we see that here are three trumps in the Tarot pack whose power is actually all about teaching you the value of *not* knowing.

'*I don't know* which one to pick. I accept whatever fate has in store for me. Chance is entertaining, and I can relax. It's not like any of it has any meaning.'

'*I don't know* where I'm going. The horses pull this thing, but I haven't a clue as to whether this image of the winner is going the same place as the horses.'

'*I don't know* what I'm seeing. I don't even know *what* to regret. In the final analysis, I don't know how much longer I can last.'

Start with '*I don't know*,' and see how far your choice, confidence, and new perspective will take you. A long way, I hope. It's in this humility that we find the power of contemplative action.

Further reading

Relevant here, for an overview of the meaning of the Tarot trumps à la ancient texts, consult the following reference book: *Explaining the Tarot: Two Italian Renaissance Essays on the Meaning of the Tarot Pack,* edited, translated and commented by Ross Sinclair Caldwell, Thierry Depaulis, and Marco Ponzi. Oxford: Maproom Publications, 2010.

LA ROVE·DE·FORTVNE

Look, the Wheel of Fortune. That means luck, right?' 'Wrong'. That's what you tell the eager ones. What you call being lucky is subject to conditions that change. What you call being unlucky is subject to conditions that change. So what's happening here? Three creatures are caught in a wheel, and they spin so fast that you can't even see their faces anymore. Is that lucky? Is that unlucky? We don't know.

But we know this:

1) If you go too fast, or for too long under conditions that dehumanize you, it's not good.
2) If you identify too much with what you're being caught up in, it's not good.
3) If you have no sense of distinct power because you're at it with everyone else, it's not good.

If you think that the previous talk about lack of agency is scary, think of this one. Here no one has agency. We don't know who turns the damn wheel. Who is behind it?

Can you ever catapult yourself off that drudgery, and become an individual again? What would it take to get your power back?

'My girlfriend wants to get married and have children right away,' a concerned young man tells you. He wants to know what married life will be like.

'It will be like hell,' I tell him, while pointing to the Wheel of Fortune.

'But... but that's a sign of being fortunate, is it not?', he insists, while also pointing to the Emperor: 'I can decide how things will go.'

'Well, you can do that,' I say to him, 'you have the power to determine when you've had enough of the routines that dehumanize you, but once caught here, in this wheel, your luck is not made if your self-empowering act ends in madness.'

I point to the Moon following the Emperor following the Wheel of Fortune. 'Marriage is not for everyone,' I say, 'and children even less, though most people would disagree. So, for you, it's hell.'

The Emperor's eyes go blank. He fancies the marriage, but the children part scares the shit out of him. A clear picture.

What's the use of imperial power if it ends in shadow, moonlight reflecting projections, and general misunderstandings? Everyone is howling and no one gets a thing. That's not your classical recipe for great fortune.

If you get caught in what you resist already, it's not enough to say that you can decide on changing the plan. If you end up carrying too much of the initial drudgery into the new plan, you can be sure that you'll reach a state where you won't even recognize yourself anymore. Who is this dog?

The Wheel of Fortune maintains some human shape. The Moon has none of that. The Moon card is the first in the sequence of trumps that features no humans in it. Why is that? What do we need to forget? Or remember? The city is still in the picture, so you're not quite in the wild yet. Who would even survive in the wild? Surely not the hopeless romantic.

Think of it in these terms: if marriage is on the table, the Wheel of Fortune is *not* a sign of fortune. If relationship is on the table, the Emperor is *not* a sign of sharing. If family is on the table, the Moon is *not* a sign of harmony.

What of agency again? If you think the cards in the previous example show problems where agency and will-power is concerned, even as we may talk about self-sacrifice, then think about the Wheel of Fortune. A nasty card where the individual is concerned. So we're back to the notion of chance. Who knows who turns the Wheel? If it's the Hanged Man, then you can wait a while. Expect nothing. If the Lovers turn your wheel, say a prayer to Cupid. You really need that luck. If the Charioteer, expect the fifth wheel to your wagon to cause some problems. If the Emperor, sigh with relief. What a break. Now something will happen. That is to say, if the Emperor can avoid going nostalgic on you, imagining too many things, or being a little afraid. Some Emperors prefer to rule over a kingdom that has no children in it, or women, or old people.

Don't think, fortune is made when spinning gold.

Don't think, power is sovereign when divided.

Don't think, fear or fascination is reality.

Your luck is made when you sit quietly, at night, and know that kings also lose their heads when the wheel turns. The thing to remember is that some cards carry the idea of agency, the power to act, while others suggest no such thing.

To assign fortune to the Wheel of Fortune would mean to assign power to it. The Wheel of Fortune has power by virtue of the power of impermanence, but impermanence is not subject to human agency and intervention. Although we may say, 'cut,' 'new rule, or 'stop that wheel', we would only be able to act in this way if the means to free others, or make offerings, were available to us. If imperial power is subject to distorted, diluted, and deluded conditions, then it acquires no more agency than the saying, 'what goes around, comes around,' which is based on observation not action.

Sometimes you have power, but get nowhere. Sometimes you don't have power, and yet you get things done. There's nothing new under the sun.

Busted Light

I F THERE'S NOTHING NEW UNDER THE SUN, a lot of things happen in the moonlight. This is because the moon craves the light of the sun. Astronomically speaking, as the moon chases after the sun, it's little wonder where we got the symbolic idea of associating the Moon with desire. The Moon, however, is a problem card because it's a natural significator for our fears and projected wishes.

The anxiety felt in the common question, 'what if I'm not good enough?' discloses both the desire to be more, and the fear of being less. But what is more and what is less? What is 'more' relative to? What is 'less' relative to?

Here comes the Sun to illuminate your speculations.

It's simple: in questions of adequacy, you only have the others to rely on. Their constitutive gazes upon you will tell you: 'yes, you're awesome,' or 'no, you can work harder on your image.' But whose truth would this be? Yours or theirs? Why do we need others to have our sense of being in the world validated? And what world are we talking about?

To give myself as an example: it would be pointless to go to the academic illuminati and expect validation for my fortune-telling skills. If they'd grant me that, they'd call it something else. We call this 'vocabulary' and being skilled at finding names for whatever disturbs us or enchants us. Likewise, it would be pointless to bring my talk of semiotics, the reading of signs, or semantics, the knowledge of how we create meaning, to the cartomantic community, even though that's exactly what I do when I read cards: I activate my semiotic and semantic vocabulary; not to mention my linguistic and grammatical competence.

The point is that when we seek validation, when we seek other people's radiance and brilliant gazes of approval on us, we must remember what tower we're in, before we get either too enthusiastic or too depressed.

NOW THINK:

What good does it do the Hermit to illuminate what the Sun already does quite as a matter of course, and much more brilliantly? To doubt what you share, the warmth and light of others, only has the function of bringing down whatever tower you're in. Over-speculation, personal crisis and weariness, run counter to the idea of an intimate relationship, of love. The

Sun is a card of love, not the Lovers. The Hermit kills it. How can you contain all that light in your little lamp? Why would you even want to do that? There's a time for the Hermit, as there's a time for the Sun, but not in that order, first the Sun and then the Hermit.

❧

'My relationship is busted,' a philosopher tells me.

'Yeah,' I say. 'Do you know why?', I ask, while looking at the Tower and just knowing already.

'Well, you know,' he says, 'she accused me of not trusting her.'

'That sounds about right to me,' I say, while looking at the Tower.

'Yeah,' the philosopher, retorts, imitating my tone, and adding irritation to it:

'How would you know what's between us?'

'I don't know,' I say. 'I'm just looking at the Tower. You wanted illuminations that you could control. On and off goes the lamp. But when the power of the Sun gets channeled through your little lamp, expect an explosion.'

❧

So it went. But the philosopher is still thinking about it. Here's one for you to think about: if you don't have enough energy for the grand love, or, if you only have energy for your own contemplative inclinations, then stay away from love that requires sharing, mutual respect, and great warmth and light.

35

The Hermit has no business stepping into the Sun, when all he wants, by virtue of his age or wisdom, is a dark cave. Here comes the Tower. But the Tower is no cave. A busted tower hit by lightening will affect everyone present in it.

If you have an inclination for solitude, then make sure you don't seek partnership or friendship. You will only contribute to bringing down the house. In a disturbing way.

Doubting the sun has rarely brought anything good with it. At best, seek shelter from it, if you find it too hot, too assuming, full of brilliance and devotion. Here comes the Sun, rising every morning, unfailingly, whether we see it or not. 'How irritating', some may think. Bottling up pressure from too much doubt and speculation is bound to find release in something that will turn into forced validation.

THE LESSON HERE IS THIS:

The ones who behold the Sun don't need to resort to sudden bursts that validate their image. The ones who behold solitude don't need others to tell them what to think. The ones who behold ruin, don't need an optimism that's not theirs.

Whether cards of relationships, warm or ruined, whether cards of solitude, imposed or self-imposed, cards tell us that we're alone. Repeat after me: *I'm alone.* When you fall from that Tower, you're alone. There may be others down with you, but you're still alone. Under the sun with another you're *alwyas* alone.

Cards tell stories of positioning. 'You are here now', they say. And so you are if you care to look, to accept what stares you in the face: light or lightning.

Sometimes You Cry

YOU DO ALL THE RIGHT THINGS, you're fair and judicious, you can let go. And still you cry. I can't remember what cards we read in my cartomancy class once, but I found myself saying something essential to one of the students who expressed slight anxiety towards my Zen attitude to all things, manifested as standing clear of emotion, avoiding over-thinking, and just breathing.

Easier said than done, as this attitude requires a lot of trust and trust is not something we grow up with. The student wanted to know about my thoughts on crying and if I ever did it. I said this to her: 'it's not a question about not crying because that's stupid, or irrelevant. Bodily sensations turn into emotions. That's a fact. The point is to be there, present, when this happens, and know exactly what your body does, which is respond, not take on a 'meaning' ride. The art is to know that this response has no meaning whatsoever. If you know that, then you stand clear of actions derived from emotion that you may be seduced into assigning meaning to.'

'Well,' I thought to myself after that tirade: 'that's pretty commonsensical. Sometimes we cry. And that's all there is to it.' Now, however, the astonishing thing is not what you hear nowadays as part of the mainstream mindfulness program that dictates: 'give yourself permission to cry.' What's astonishing is that when you sometimes cry, you do so as part of your default nature, not as part of any program dictating anything, even when this program is deemed superior to other programs.

I'm thoroughly amused when I hear it all the time: 'give yourself permission to cry.' 'Give yourself permission to yell.' 'Give yourself permission to love yourself.' 'Give yourself permission to not feel shame. There's nothing to be ashamed of.' One grows ever so tired of all these permissions. One grows ever so tired of all self-empowering speech. Why can't we accept the fact that when sometimes we cry, we do so because *that's all there is to it?* Why can't people get it that this line, *because that's all there is to it*, is enough.

Giving permission, even if that be myself embodying the ultimate self-empowering agency, 'I, and I mean, *I* [double stress here] give myself permission to…' smacks too much of culture, vulnerability as a commodity, the culture that now dictates: 'be good to yourself, love yourself, don't give any fucks, refute all critique, you're perfect.' This is all good and sound advice, if only all this self-love would not be so god damn intangible. As in the case with our example of knowing what the heart wants in order to follow it commonsensically, we also want to ask here: what is the premise for the self-love, for the perfection of self in its imperfection? It's not like we exist in a vacuum. We exist in the eyes of the beholder.

Someone comes to me, looks at her cards, and starts crying. Sobbing she says: 'I do all the right things, I'm fair and judicious, and I can let go. And yet, the woman with the sword here makes me cry'.

If I were to express an opinion, I'd say I can only agree that any woman with a sword in her hand should make us cry, but I'm here to do more than express an opinion. I'm here to point to three cards, full of woman-power, and how we can understand the process of going for it and getting it, formalizing it, and then changing lanes. How do *you* understand this? What happens to your royal consecrations, your degrees and professional confidence, when the truth is that sometimes you cry, you spill your waters, and hope to God that your naked body can behold all that star power coming down on you, while you're out in the woods, away from the city and its masks and costumes?

You see, it's when we see these good cards on the table, each embodying very different functions, that we understand the meaning of the phrase, 'and that's all there is to it'. What does giving yourself permission for anything have to do with anything? Could we please just see things as they are, and perhaps stop enjoying our lamenting syndromes for nothing? No one is truly supported in their indulgence of shallow thinking.

Sometimes, when you're done with your duties, you go home and take a bath, and that's all there is to it. Why does this need further explanation? Conversely, why does, 'sometimes we cry' need explanation? Why do we need to sentence ourselves to the latest phrase in vogue? Why bring in injunctions that we pass on ourselves even when they are inappropriate? 'Give yourself permission to feel bad. That's a good girl.'

We're only in the courthouse if we see ourselves needing a courthouse. But are courthouses home? They are not. They are cold and impartial. They are not exactly a place for pleasure: 'give yourself permission to drink more wine, before you sign the divorce papers here.' In a more radical context, what if the truth is that there is never any need for anything?

Don't think, 'here comes the Empress, the nurturing and clever woman.' What if she's just clever, or just nurturing sitting on shit you don't even want to come close to?

Don't think, 'here comes Justice, the woman of method, she's going to win my case.' What if she's the Devil's advocate in a nurturer's costume, or no costume, holding only a promise for deliverance?

Don't think, 'here comes the Star, all my sins can be washed away. I can give myself permission to sin some more.'

Sometimes you cry. Sometimes your crying is completely independent of your permissions and feelings you have and feelings you think you *should* have. Now you're welcome to ask: is there a difference? No, there isn't. Your feelings are just thoughts in your head. Your feelings are words and language;

the language that the Empress speaks, that Justice formalizes, and that the Star sings.

Your language is never yours. Your thoughts are never yours. Your feelings are never yours. Even your body that you think is yours is a prisoner of your language of desire. Tragic. If you think you can replace the reality of this with more dogma, concepts, and embodied identifications, then the tragedy is twice as tensioned, as the premise for its event is anchored in plain delusion.

Sometimes all the good cards that have a good message for you can still make you cry, and that's all there is to it.

What's In A Name?

WHAT IS A TEACHER GOOD FOR, if she can't participate in resolving conflict? In my 20 years of teaching experience this question almost became a mantra. But addressing conflict is not always free of conflict. The reason for this is because we live through perceptions. You may think you're doing all the right things, you may think you possess fairness and are capable of generosity – as seen in the previous example when the Empress, Justice, and the Star got together – and yet you may find that what you do is also perceived by others as dominance, discipline, and overbearing.

Who is right and who is wrong? This question is big enough to create conflict and tension in the body. Tension in the body manifests as illness and a sense of heaviness. On the intangible and unconscious level, as you feel your heart is hard, you start wondering how to make it soft again. In spiritual contexts such as Buddhism, softening the heart is a primary aim. A soft heart gives you access to equanimity and flow. But what does having a soft heart mean? What does being in the flow mean?

If you have a spiritual adviser or mentor you consult, you may hear this message: 'you channel a lot of demons. Cut it out.' If you have a family doctor or a psychologist you consult, you may hear this message: 'you're addicted. You give in to obsession. Cut it out.' A Pope, Devil, Death situation.

Often this advice comes in response to the question on the table about how to solve conflict. Fair enough. But when the conflict is inner, felt at the heart level, then this question, while on the table, remains either inarticulate, or difficult to formulate.

Why is this so? Because of what we call the unconscious. The best way I can think of explaining the unconscious is to point to how the process of acquiring a sense of self occurs. This is a big area, and each discipline, from psychoanalysis to neuroscience, has different things to say about it.

THINK OF IT IN THIS WAY:

After several attempts at recognizing what you are — when you realize already at infant level that you're not exactly your mother, the one you mirror yourself into — something obvious hits you: *you are your name.* Not only that, but you realize also that if you don't like this name, you can just change it.

The latter is considered a form of adolescent rebellion, and it's interesting to observe, but the process of 'selfing' is the same, boiling down to this realization: *you are your name.* You're conscious of what that means because you're always in the process of branding your name, selling it, transacting with it, negotiating with it and for it. You may finish an education, but it's not you who gets the degree and a diploma. It's your name that gets recognition. You take this name and plaster it all over job applications, and eventually you get to pop the champagne. But what gets celebrated is your name, not you.

So far so good. You're now conscious of *what* you are, not *who* you are. But then something else happens. Freud would say, welcome to your death drive. Your instincts rule. You're way more than your conscious name. Lacan, Freud's main interpreter would say, your unconscious is language, a borrowed thing. You are a 'thing' of chance.

Neuroscientists such as Candace Pert would say, your unconscious is your body. Medical doctors would say, your unconscious sits in your gut. The gut has an intelligence that the conscious mind does not.

We can't escape the simple fact that the body beholds our brain and the mind. But consciousness itself seems to be outside of the body, some say. We now enter the woo territory.

You start obsessing already: who is this 'I' beyond the name? That's a very good question. A true question. One of the Devil's favorites, because it creates conflict.

Time to bring in the exorcists.

If you're brave enough, or had the good fortune to come across a teacher who enlightens you on the spot: 'relax, soften your heart, nothing has substance, you're nothing', then you can say hello to Death and stop channeling the demons of your existential crisis.

When we think of the Popes of the world as spiritual teachers, exorcists, counselors, or medical doctors, what we think of is a name: 'this one can fix it,' we think, as we spill our guts while the clock is ticking. Tick, tock, tick, tock. 'Isn't he done with that blessing yet? All that patronizing…'

But you keep going. You fill the good doc with your obsessions, if you can even articulate them, and then you hear the verdict: 'nothing can save you but death. Either you cut the crap, or you wait until you die.'

The good news is that nothing lasts forever. The bad news is the nothing lasts forever. This is a good meme that circulates in public consciousness. Enjoying your symptoms, clinging to emotion or intellect, will only get you so far. Manipulating others into believing your stories, or your change of names, will only make them say: 'off with your head; we're so done with this'.

THE LESSON TO PONDER HERE IS THIS:

Don't think that only the competent ones with a name and reputation can solve a conflict. They can, but it would require intense listening on your part. If you happen to channel demons, then your focus will be elsewhere, on your addiction, aversion, compulsion, worry, envy, jealousy, and so on.

Don't think that your inner demons are cool, simply because you heard someone say that the Devil represents passion, attraction, and cunningness. It can, but in a way that demonstrates restlessness and a disconnect between the body and regular peace of mind. Your unconscious is the Devil you don't know.

Don't think that putting an end to your clinging is a tragedy. It hurts to remember that 'remembering your name' means exactly nothing, but it's worth remembering it nonetheless.

NOW CONSIDER THIS:

'When the student is ready, the teacher will appear,' the Indian saying goes that some attribute to the Buddha. You are ready when your heart is soft. You're ready when the Devil you know is *not* unconsciously the Devil you actually don't know but serve, one way or another. Just listen.

When the Pope's finger goes up, it's not always as a blessing. It's a gesture that can point to many things. It can point to you and your unconscious demons, not just your name given in baptism, the name Death will help you inscribe on a tombstone. As dead, you're of little use to the living. Keep alive, and ask for your name that only your gut knows, your unconscious knows, and your body knows.

What *you* know is nothing. The only thing you can know with some degree of certainty is that you're here now, breathing, reading these words. But the Devil will convince you that you know everything already. And if you *feel* that you don't know it, the 'all,' he will promise to give it to you. Ay, the pacts many have made in exchange for knowledge…

We all know how those stories end, with the big essential-izer, Death, laughing at you, as you're clinging to your name, the one you *know* you have, because the Devil himself gave it to you, in a darker baptism.

Further reading

For a heavily Freudian influenced Tarot interpretation, see Alejandro Jodorowsky's, *The Way of the Tarot* (2009). Destiny Books. For inspiration on how the body acts as your unknown territory, see Candace Pert's, *Your Body Is Your Subconscious Mind* (2004). Sounds True Publishing.

I F YOU GO FROM 1 TO 21, disregarding the other steps even if they don't come in their ordinary numerical order, you may discover that in the process you've just managed to lose your breath. Having the skills to do something is one thing. Having the skills to survive while you're at it is another thing.

Magic work, which the interpretative art always is, begins with a moment of enchantment. First, you look over your shoulder to make sure no one is after you. Next, you *inspirit* yourself. You conjure forces with your mind, and then off you go to tell a story. You can say to yourself: 'now I will enchant the world.'

You can take the necessary steps for preparation, and then test what there is to test: is there an interest in this thing? Am I giving others what they what to hear, or serve because I'm the best at it and can't help it?

There's always a public out there. In fact, without the others we would never get a sense of what home means, or what being familiar with something means. But it doesn't follow that just because you're familiar with something, you're also familiar with what the public wants. It may well be the public wants a package solution, the key to all the problems in the world, but when we talk about raised consciousness, what we talk about is not second-guessing what kind of judgments go into holistic approaches. The Magician may be well versed in selling his tricks to the public, but without maintaining a resilient mind, a mind that focuses by de-concentrating, he will never be able to get past a mere promise.

As a writer, I get to read a lot of writing-related correspondence, including campaigns inviting me to join this or that writing class. I also see a lot of talking heads… about writing. I always consider taking a new class, even though teaching writing and creative writing is something I've done myself. I like to learn new things. But I can tell you this: I never embark on a course that describes its implicit premise in this way:

Hey there Camelia,
So. You've had struggles. Big ones.
Debt. Addiction.

Raised by mean chimpanzees who didn't share their bananas with you. But you overcame those obstacles, found self-love, and now you're living the life of your dreams!

– Marie Forleo selling The Copy Cure

Now, I get this enchantment. I get that this is an invitation to consider just how easy it is to find a topic to write about, and sell, as it's something that already stares you in the face. Writing is, after all, just a craft. But what I don't get is the insistence that the person behind these words, addressing me 'directly,' knows me, knows my story, understands me deeply, and is willing to show compassion. Now that's a whole lot of knowledge in one basket. About an other you don't know.

The main question that begs itself here is this one: what is it that marketers are missing when they act on assumption? When they 'know' everything about the people they want to sell to? How do they know what they know? Because of statistics? Demographics? Honest to god wisdom? Analytics of what works and what doesn't? I'd say that what is missing is stamina and resilience. The very ingredients that give confidence. Confidence is not your shining armor. It's your faith and trust in your dexterity, finger work coupled with robust demonstrations. Confidence is zero tricks.

Why am I suspicious of the way *The Copy Cure* sells? Let it be said that I don't doubt the value of a product I don't know, so I don't comment on the content that may very well be both valuable and well put together. What I want to know is what makes seemingly competent people, who may have a good product in their hands, resort to tricks that are anything but robust.

As it happens, I never had big struggles. I was never in debt. I was never addicted, and I was never raised by mean chimpanzees who didn't share their bananas with me. I never had to overcome obstacles, find self-love, and live the life of my dreams.

To be sure, there's a good, vivid image here that hooks. I can just picture the bananas that I didn't get to eat, even though that has never been my story. I fail, however, to fall for debt and addiction because these are words that operate with an intangible sense of victimhood. While some may find themselves nodding, 'yeah, man, I've been there and it sucked,' I don't feel moved by generalities.

What I'm trying to say is that without doing the footwork, merely pressing on the button that we call 'share your vulnerable story' will only get you to where you bedazzle a whole lot of people with content devoid of content.

JUST THINK:

What good is a con man who sells you the world, but teaches you nothing about the world? What good is a con man who enchants you, but has no solid skills for anything?

Don't think that just because a magician is in the picture, he is also able to magic your world in a way that's useful to you.

Don't think that just because something is popular, it's also the best. When the clarion's call heralds an opinion, this opinion is not fair judgment or discernment.

Don't think that just because many fall for it, the world that's offered also matches the world that's promised.

When the Magician works for me in a world that's full of fanfare and wonder, he represents something that an athlete knows: focus and stamina.

Focus and stamina as a resilience pack is created in the mind. You can instruct the mind to be in the body, stay there and forget about its thoughts, positive or negative. You can instruct the magician who wants to get there fast to remember to listen, focus and concentrate. But where is this point of focus when you deal with the public, with people having different needs? How can you listen to them all? What world do you promise or herald for them all?

❦

Russian scientists call this process of holistic awareness 'attention deconcentration', when your focus is on distributed attention, when your focus is on the margins of everything, including the center, but not *on* the center, not *on* the dot.

Free diver and water magician Natalia Molchanova, now vanished from this world while giving a private deep diving lesson, referred to her skills as being the skills of a warrior, a samurai, and one might add, a great Zen master. A magician who is also a warrior, who is so good that he simply kills every trick he ever does, can create a world of magic out of empty consciousness, the consciousness that goes into a magic trick beyond the trick.

This is exactly what we find in the time it takes to go from 1 to 21: empty consciousness. Imagine approaching the public, the witnesses to your dexterous skills, from this emptiness, from a space that's completely free of judgment, personal involvement, and emotional distraction.

Can you focus on your world's edges and its guarded corners, and from this focus let your skills emerge as universal, yet addressing each and every one in the excited crowd you wish to touch with your enchantment? Moreover, what is the premise for your touch?

People are waiting for this, for your resilient and robust skills, not for resounding blah blah. You can be the secret agent bringing liberation to the ones ready for a new world. If you can do that, enchant through skill and pedagogy, you will find that you don't need to use words or gestures as tools for expressing generalities. You will use words and gestures to create pure worlds of magic, worlds that awaken your and others' awareness beyond anything you can ever imagine.

Further reading

For inspiration from the fascinating world of focus and attention, see *The Deepest Dive* by Alec Wilkinson, in *The New Yorker.* August 24, 2009.

Give Yourself Time

SOME WOULD ARGUE that the highest human art is knowing how to avoid transforming your anger into aggression. Just imagine life not being about strategies of coping, but rather about avoiding events: avoiding an accident, if you're driving; avoiding twisting your ankle, if you're walking; avoiding running out of lamp oil, if you're seeking things in the dark; avoiding getting sunburnt, if you're out in the garden playing all day; avoiding domination, if you're trying to persuade others; avoiding indifference, if you're suspended; avoiding fear, if you're out camping in the wild. Are you noticing all the trumps right in this line?

Some would say, living a life of caution is a boring life. But what if caution is wise? What if caution is exciting because its highest expression is moderation and perfect balance? Imagine being perfectly balanced and thus able to maintain perfect peace of mind. I know that peace of mind seduces the hell out of me. Peace of mind exerts magnetic power over me. It makes me write tomes of poetry, all having titles that carry the word 'grace' in them. Peace of mind 'thinks' nothing of struggle. It writes aggression off. If there's anger, it just flows. There's no coercion.

Much of the Buddhist teaching that fascinates me stresses the importance of knowing this, actually rather subtle, difference between anger and aggression.

Chögyam Trungpa Rinpoche built a whole empire by talking about this, about the art of rising to your angry self, and then giving it a lesson in radical acceptance. We are grateful to such masters.

Anger is good, aggression is bad. We use 'good' and 'bad' here instrumentally, not because we believe in such division, but because it helps us understand what is at stake when dealing with beasts, with the ones who never seem to be on the same page with us.

First you fight with them, then you try to instruct them by the book in the high art of showing some discretion – no bullies, thank you – and then you go the diplomatic way, smoothing the relation. Compromise is also a high art, but only if you can manage your resentment. Without such skill, you end up with a flow of hatred rather than a flow of peace.

When Force shows up, trying to overpower the problem in front of her, the Popesse following her keeps a record. In the process of describing the problem, you give yourself time to see if you get it right. How big is the problem exactly? What nature does it have?

Giving yourself time is also a high art. Giving yourself time to ask the question of what the purpose of anything is opens the gate to flow, to balance, to a perfect mix of the beast with the book.

Just think:

When Force, the Popess, and Temperance show up in this particular order, they invite you to consider these questions: what are the strategies of coping with force? Anger operates with force, with physical and mental strength, and with impulsivity, the opposite of resilience. Impulsivity that lingers turns into stubbornness, and there's a short road from there to bullying. Can you cultivate your anger? What book will be your good book? The one you go to every time you need to solve a conflict? I go to popular sayings and proverbs. I find folk wisdom the best. New knowledge about anger management can be fascinating, and it can crack some skulls, but it never beats the common sense that folk wisdom has.

Don't just assume that the card of Strength is a representation of your power in unmediated form. No one can handle raw power.

Don't just assume that the card of the Popess is your wisdom in unmediated form. No one is wise without experience.

Don't just assume that the card of Temperance is your healer in unmediated form. No one heals without first understanding the root of a problem.

My practice of contemplating with the Tarot cards, trumps and pip cards included, has always been a practice anchored in getting a sense of how things flow, or don't.

It takes time to figure out the power of flow. It takes time to figure out how you can transform what makes you tick like a bomb into listening to the pulse of your heart: does your pulse match the pulse of the earth?

Perhaps this is the reason why influential occultists of the 19th century thought of the card of Temperance as a card of time, a card that blends our perception of past, present, and future, making temporality a matter of unity, not of distinct separations. P.D. Ouspensky's book, *The Symbolism of the Tarot,* even insists that Temperance is time, not the Hermit, another favorite contender for time. 'The name of the angel is Time,' he says, 'time in its most incomprehensible aspect.'

The premise for this observation is the fact that time doesn't flow in one direction only. It flows both ways, in and out of perspective. If you can crack a problem by understanding its nature, you will see how flow makes everything transparent. You will see the invisible, and understand the silent gaping of the mouth.

Your *Ahhh* is waiting to be born, of ink and feather, words flowing from your pen, flying on your page, saying, 'give yourself time.' Give yourself time, and you will understand the subtle burst of the mystery of the obvious.

Although I read cards following the method of paying attention to the visual language of the cards at the formal level, which is to say that I look at color and design and then embodiment, function, gesture, and voice, I appreciate the poetic voice of the occultists when they describe the Tarot cards in terms of their participation in the transmission of mystery traditions. Hence I recommend P.D. Ouspensky's *The Symbolism of the Tarot: Philosophy of Occultism in Pictures and Numbers*. Dover Publications, 1976.

For my own take, see my related books: *Marseille Tarot: Towards the Art of Reading*. EyeCorner Press, 2014, and *What is Not: Marseille Tarot à la Carte*, EyeCorner Press, 2019. For a dash of cards and magic, see *The Oracle Travels Light: Principles of Magic with Cards*. EyeCorner Press, 2015.

For common sense wisdom, see Chögyam Tungpa Rinpoche's *Shambala: The Scared Path of the Warrior*. Shambala Publications, 1984.

WE LIVE IN A WORLD OF REPRESENTATIONS. We transact with the notion of a 'self' against 'the other.' A zen inclined person is able to maintain the fixity of such social constructs, while at the same time know that they are precisely that, social constructs. Part of what I like about my work as a fortuneteller is seeing how we cope with the perennial question of the self in relation, and the point when the idea of taking everything personally breaks down. I'm after that point, because recognizing the flow of events in the proposition that life happens as it happens features absolutely no constructs of separation: I against the other, mother against daughter, friend against enemy, groups marked by identity against governments.

There are many questions to pose when divisions and separations are maintained. There are no questions to pose when the point of break down of social constructs occur. The first thing that goes out with the rubble is precisely representation. It's a tough one to handle, because we all want recognition. We want recognition for what we do, and we want recognition of our boundaries.

If the neighbor parks their car on my property because it's convenient for them, as there's so much more space I enjoy over here, you can be sure that I'll react. The fact that I have more space than the other is besides the point, and none of the other's business. What I want is not a false correlation about what I own and why — I don't even owe any explanations for that — but a simple recognition of my jurisdiction. The whole legal system is built around policing the self in relation.

The same applies to work. I read the cards for people who ask about how to deal with the situation when they present an original idea at work, only to see other colleagues run off with it without crediting. As it happens, cards for divination have been invented to address precisely such situations, when the dividing line between taking liberties and maintaining boundaries is blurred. In all my divination books and cartomancy courses, I dedicate entire sections and sessions to the art of the question, the gist of it being that it's a good idea to identify first what is at stake in a question, and then proceed to analysis and judgment.

As questions can assume different characters — such as the descriptive, the analytical, the reflective, and the evaluative — they can also change nuance, all according to how the shifting signifiers or the representational enters into play across the board. The question 'does he love me', invites to a description of the situation on the basis of which you can conclude either in the affirmative, the negative, or the 'maybe' mode. 'How he loves me' invites to a reflection of modality on the basis of which I can then conclude in the evaluative: 'he loves me like this, serving me coffee and kissing me when I expect it the least, so he's worth keeping.' 'Why he loves me like he does' invites to a reading that has an investigative character. Let's just say that by merely being aware of these four types of questions we commonly encounter in our work with the cards, we get to see how entertaining fortune-telling is. Now, what of the time when we don't have a question to bring to the cards? Since the 60s and up until recently, when people started looking at the cards as markers for something other than a psychological process, reading cards according to their nominal quality was very popular. Knowing how 'this means that' settled it for many, and it still does, when we look at the popularity of reading 'a daily', that is to say, when we look at how one card can stand as a predictive representation of how the events in a day will unfold.

You can say: 'today I got the Hermit. This means that I'll be off Facebook.' In this reading of the Hermit, what I do is look at the function of what we culturally associate with the Hermit, the act of retreating from the world. This is good enough for me, but I see that there are many for whom looking at the function of things is not enough. They want *meaning,* as there's *more* to the cards than

just straightforward function. There's symbolic function and value. There's story. 'Give me that,' the ones invested in delusions ask. So people launch in a discourse that's purely nominally descriptive on an elastic that stretches from the commonsensical to the utterly ridiculous. Any classic little white book, the short booklet that accompanies a standard set of cards, will introduce you to a list of keywords that you can pick from, for instance these associations: the Hermit equals old age, aloneness, retreat from the world, wisdom, prudence, attention, mistrust, illness, lack of vigor, stupor, amnesia, and so on. Now, there's nothing wrong with such a list of words, if there's a question on the table, but things go rotten when there's no question. The Hermit representing ten different things is a whole lot of things to equalize, so how do you determine which of the ten will turn out to represent your day? You can't. Not if you want precision. You can only do it in hindsight: 'ah yes, it was all about being limited in my body, as my back hurt today; it was not at all about sitting and philosophizing.' There goes that initial insight in your 'daily'...

I think about questions a lot, and I like to be prompted by some that are not necessarily those of my common conditioning. If you haven't noticed yet, most of the questions that I've come up with for this first part of the book are prompted by real questions and events that we can all experience. At the same time, in my going about getting an answer from the cards, I also let the cards inspire me towards honing in on what's already on my mind. We call this 'fine-tuning the question.' This is the situation when I don't just look at the cards to read for the plot, for 'meaning', as arbitrary meanings leave me cold and not convinced. I don't read for the pragmatic function of our cultural competence in recognizing what images represent exactly either. I read for both the answer and the art of the question itself, especially when I look at the cards past conditioning. The only condition I take into account is the framing of the context.

Essentially, all questions are the same, as they spring from desire. We may call this desire 'need' or, on occasion, 'passion' or 'fancy,' but upon finer analysis we'll see that what we call 'need' is very much subject to desire, with desire ruling over all the other names. The predictive question, 'will the plumber come today to fix the kitchen pipes?' is no different than philosophizing on whether you'll be open for an intimate encounter with the plumber, in spite of the fact that you know already that he's married. You can ask, 'to what extent is it legitimate to give in to the fancy of bringing the plumber from the kitchen, where he is needed, to the bedroom, where he is not?' and in this asking discover that you've just framed the question around a new context for your desire that has zero to do with any moral judgment.

What I see too often in the cartomantic world is a readiness to judge the question. 'Psychologizing the self is out,' some proclaim, and then declare that we're now with a new fortune-telling eon, and therefore we should only stick to the plumbing questions. That's the trend, and we don't want to mess with the trends. But what if I want to fuck the plumber, as I agonize badly about it, my soul gone to pieces? Oh, I can't go to the fortuneteller with this because this is not the 60s anymore... Enough of all that libertarian hippiedom. I should only ask if I can score the job as an accountant... where the plumber works.

The world is full of thieves of our common sense and sense of discrimination. Beyond polemics, I wish more 'critics' invested in offering uninformed opinions could hear themselves, before they all pontificate on what questions we can, should, must, or avoid to ask. There's little virtue in being an idiot. We may think of that, especially since, as it happens, the Tarot has been built around the representation of classical virtues, with justice, fortitude, temperance, and prudence leading the way. Always depending on context, the nominal factor here acquires significance only if we constrain the question to fit a template, a trifecta, a four-point model, or a 12-step program.

How do we ask questions that bring us to a level where we get to experience something other than a trite model? People love models, and I'm good at crafting and designing them myself for instrumental purpose, but when I want to go past representations, and get a sense of how I can better observe flow not separation, then I must find a way of asking questions that bring me to a place where I don't operate with opposites: esoteric Tarot vs. fortunetelling, moral judgment vs. whoredom, sins vs. virtues, 'me' against 'the other'. The classicists didn't have a 'bad' category for the autobiographical self, rather more like elevate it to the status of ultimate virtue – 'being yourself' is very much endorsed as a virtue right now – but upon reflecting on the actual construction of 'myself,' what can we say we find there? I say 'reflecting,' because that's my preferred mode of reading the cards, more via philosophical inquiry and less via psychological observation.

I'm asking the full deck of cards now, since I'm ready to introduce you to the essentials in reading with the pip and court cards, just to give you a quick taste for it. The Queen of Coins, 2 Swords, and the Charioteer made an appearance.

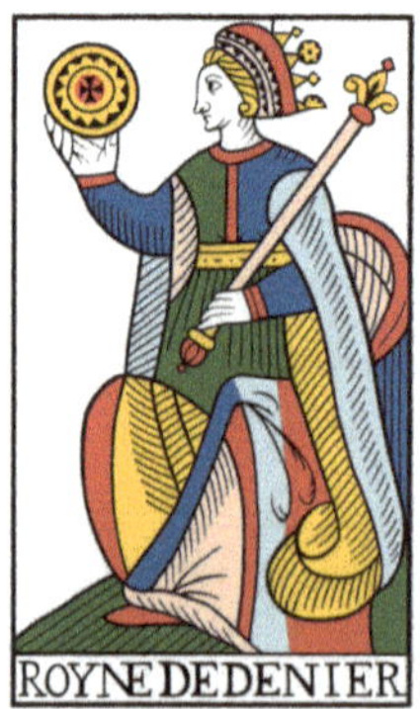

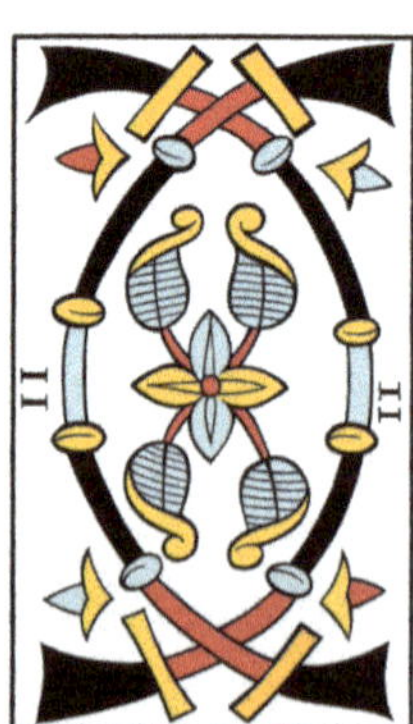

We can go like this: 'mirror, mirror on the wall, what I am seeing here? I'm so conflicted. Is the self all an armor? Fast horses? An emblazoned inscription? Mirror, mirror in my hand, what are you saying? I feel the swords against my back. Two swords, two horses… If only the swords were cups, then we could all drink something to my honor, to the crown on my head. I worked so hard for it. My relation with 'the other' is tensioned. We speak the same language, have our eyes on the ball, or some ball, but the other is more eager. I just want to sit here for an answer. But the cold blades… I'm not even sure who is more hurt. All this competition. *Myself* as a competition. Maybe I'm tired of winning. There's always an 'other,' younger and more interesting, ready to take my place. Let them. Soon they'll sit with a mirror of their own…'

French poet Arthur Rimbaud is famous for this phrase: 'I is another.' What a clever man he was! I see that what the cards are saying is exactly this, 'I is another,' one I'm always in relation to, compete with. But for what? The relatable? The mirror is empty. The mirror has always been empty. This is what the fortuneteller knows. We read the cards for this knowledge. Nothing more, nothing less. If you're adventurous, you can find that a snappy *and* thoughtful reading under the signature of *Read like the Devil* is more dangerous than all the questions in the world. Go ahead and pose them. All the questions are marvellous. If you're lucky, you can arrive at a true question to pose to the cards, that is to say, one that doesn't involve the clock or imagining what you will do to the dashing plumber once he shows up. A true question springs from the sincere heart, a heart that doesn't need an empty mirror to check with.

The Power of the Pips

WHEN THE SERIES of eight lectures *The Power of the Trumps* was released in both video and book form, it was received with great applause. 'This is not just about cards, this is about life and a lot more,' people said, gradually expressing what became a consensus opinion.

People are right. My work with the cards is not about cards for the sake of history, aesthetics, or even divination practices, but about 'life and more,' simply because there's great attention that goes into figuring out how images on cardboard participate in expanding our field of habitual thinking beyond cultural dictations.

'This is not just about cards, this is about life and a lot more,' is thus a statement about what happens when we read cards in context, which is to say, when we anchor our interpretations in a specific question related to a specific situation. The range of questions can also vary, from the very concrete and mundane, to the metaphysical and philosophical. Some would call the latter a waste of time, frowning also upon the possibility to psychologize the self – again, a popular practice once upon a time in the 60s, now fallen in disrepute. But as I'm never here to judge the question, I'd say that as long as we use the cards to get a kick in our imagination, the only thing we need to worry about is the extent to which we either read the damn cards, or use them to talk about all things irrelevant to life and thought.

Now, what can we say about reading the pip cards, the number cards devoid of figurative images representing people 'doing' life? What do we do about all that geometry and gardening, judging by the arrangement of elements in our stylized suits, with coins, cups, batons, and swords crossing each other or running parallel, embellished also in their 'action' by vine leaves or other floral suggestions?

What about the ever-contradictory theories about the court cards as aspects of ourselves, archetypes, or as extensions of standard human behavior, ranging from the embodiments of critics and abusers to healers and heroes? My theory is that the power of the minor arcana of the tarot is all about courting. Whether we like it or not, we're all seduced by the abstractness of numbers and by the desired identity that the court cards can offer us. Who doesn't fancy herself as a mean Queen of Spades, if your practice has any occult leanings? Who doesn't fancy himself as a man of cunning resource, sitting solidly on a whole bank, and affording the luxury of generosity? I have as yet to see a magician who thinks poverty is part of the practice. There are exceptions, of course, when the magician is a monk, but that's rare.

In this part of the book we look at the ways in which the pip cards have a story to tell that's all their own. As I've written before on the basic method of reading the pip and court cards in my book, *Marseille Tarot: Towards the Art of Reading* (2014), I will not repeat here what I said there. Here I want to present you with a similar approach to reading cards in context as demonstrated in the first part dealing with the trumps.

This means that there's a specific idea that guides my reading, either based on a concrete question, or one that springs from a troubling matter or concern. The idea is to give you something to think about, while also giving you a specific model for how you can approach reading the pip cards.

As mentioned already, my preferred method is to teach by example. If I have a theory, I give it to you in the form of an example. Because we have two different types of cards that compose the so-called minor arcana of the Marseille Tarot, number cards and court cards, I will first introduce you briefly to the principles of strategy of reading the pip cards, and then offer as well an ampler discussion of what to make of the court cards. What we're after is to set up a playful and spontaneous approach to the pip cards, while at the same time keep an eye on a strict, yet useful method. This approach consists of reading strings of three cards or more, as they connect to what we often encounter in life situations, whether of mundane or more metaphysical character.

In terms of style, you can expect to see here the same approach to cartomancy that I also like to associate with the idea of martial arts, or going for the clean cut. This is another way of saying that I read the cards like the Devil, aiming for the kind of penetrating insight that is even beyond any settled negotiation. We don't argue with what stares us in the face.

This is a stringent approach to the spontaneous, in the sense that what I have to offer is very much anchored in deconstructing — Zen style — language, clichés, mainstream opinions, and other 'natural' approaches to thinking. My sole aim is to make you go: 'why didn't I think of this before?'

Knowing all your cards, trumps, pips, and courts, is knowing how to string together a narrative that makes sense in terms of coherence and cohesiveness. In other words, knowing your cards is knowing what makes you a good diviner; a diviner that's not invested in borrowed lists of meanings, comparison, fear of inadequacy, or strategies of compensating for the lack of personal nerve and original voice.

What makes a good diviner is this: knowing that the cards are a perfect mirror. A perfect mirror is not truth. People come to ask a question. That's all they do. Ask a question. They put their involved issues in front of an empty mirror. You don't 'help' them. You let the mirror reflect the deep and hidden answers. You are reliable in your practice. You say: 'this is your story. It ends like this.' If you stick to that, you'll be able to enjoy the ride with the power of the pip cards here, all about courting YOU and your skills in seeing the obvious. As I'm not into revolutions, or into revealing the 'ultimate secret' to how to read the pip cards, what I hope to achieve is to give you a sense of how magical your readings can be, if you simply purse the straightforward only.

A *Short Theory of the Pip Cards*

I N OUR WORK WITH THE CARDS, we talk about nothing other than connection and path-work, ways to connect, ways to reconnect if disconnection happens, and so on. Especially the pip cards emphasize connection. In contrast, the trumps have a stronger individual force, where we actually see that the reason why the trumps are strong and appear individual is because 'connection' is already part of the program. Connection is not raised to higher status, when it already has high status.

Think about that. Think about the Emperor and how he relates to connecting. Do you think that the Emperor needs liking, before he goes on to give directives or delegate whatever there is to be done? Historically, there have been Emperors obsessed with having people like them — think of Nero — but that has always proven to be the wrong approach.

All narcissists and others who merely claim super-connecting powers, yet demonstrate the opposite, end up beheaded or in the ditch. Why? Because they don't get connection; because they completely misunderstand what connection is essentially, namely, that it is all pervasive and encompassing.

You can never *not* connect. This is the subtle message of the pips cards. A pip card next to the Emperor who fulfils the function of leadership will talk about the ways in which leadership comes across in connective ways that underlie a specific structure.

In the first part of this book on the power of the trumps I've written about the subtle power of these cards, but where the pips are concerned, what I find utterly fascinating is the fact that, when the suits connect to the function of the trumps, or simply interconnect when no trumps are in the picture, what they do is teach a lesson in temporal and spatial awareness.

What I'm saying is this: all pip cards can be understood in terms of how we also understand temporal and spatial metaphors in a structural, binary, and numerical order: inside/outside, up/down, far/near, strong/soft, fast/slow, here/there, a little/a lot, sharp/dull, moveable/immovable, and so on – and yes, the latter, 'and so on' is also very much a representative of what pip cards can also act as: conjunctions, appositions, pauses, ellipses, and adjectival and adverbial modifiers, including objections of this type: 'yes, but', and so on.

We tend to think that cards are invested with symbolic power. This is true to some extent, as there's no relation that we experience that's not already symbolic. Symbolism happens by default, through language. Language is representative of thoughts, not reality. It is also made up of random glyphs, not divine words. Your very act of getting up in the morning, taking a shower, putting some perfume on and donning your best costume is a symbolic act of your readiness to go out and conquer the world. You think that if you do this regularly, it will pay off and you end up belonging. But how is this thinking representative of reality, of *what* and *who* you are? It's not. All symbolic acts rest on dictations, not awareness of original beingness.

Now, the difference between a symbol and a connector is that while a connector pervades what is the case, a symbol serves a master, as its whole premise rests on cultural convention. A symbol doesn't arise out of vacuum. Someone creates it and then convinces others of its value. This is all fine until the point when this value is passed on as the thing itself, as reality. While some eat it raw, others resist.

In my work with the cards I see myself participating in this act of resisting. We use symbols to manipulate with emotions. Who stands to gain from this? I try to address this question in a detached way, and then look at what other strategies for communication we have available to us that do not rely on a system of transacting with clichés.

The trumps tell us what is at stake. The pip cards make clear the connection between the agents involved and the way a narrative or story unfolds temporally and sequentially. Let me give an example: symbolically, for some, the Magician connects man to the divine. If your cards are the popular Waite-Smith Tarot you will nod to this, as this correspondence is part of the standard interpretation of the Magician. For others this connection is something that the Pope takes care of. Symbolically, some connect the batons with fire, the coins with earth, the swords with thoughts, and the cups with water. I prefer my batons connected to air, as they tend to stick up in the wind, coins with fire, as you can't get one that's not forged in heat, swords with the earth as they can dig it too after the stabbing is done and the corpse needs burying. The cups are pretty much a given, being obviously associated with all forms of liquids and libations, from blood to wine.

Functionally, however, we can see how we can bypass the symbolic constraint if we simply stick to noting what the suits do as a matter of course. In terms of connection, I like to think of the four suits as representing bridges, the space between here and there. In photography this space is called 'negative space,' the space where light meets darkness and shadows are created. Think of how each of the four Aces initiates a suit, and represents a bridge over the negative space, the space without which there would be no primordial act.

THE ACE OF COINS is the message: there is life and death. The more you cultivate both, the more polished you are.

THE ACE OF CUPS is the shape of formlessness. Without flow resistance wins.

THE ACE OF BATONS is the silent wind. It pushes you over into acceptance.

THE ACE OF SWORDS is the void of expectation. When the mind is free, the bones can create.

When we consider the pip cards as connectors, as bridges over troubled waters, we realize that what we once took as primary symbolic power is now turned over to the subtle realm, where the ambiguity of the symbol, to always mean more than it purports, is left to its own ambivalent device. No more drama. With this sense of a symbol in mind consider these relations:

> YES/NO (red card/black card)
> A LITTLE / A LOT (1, 10)
> BIG/SMALL (King, Page)
> UP/DOWN (10, Ace)
> INSIDE/OUTSIDE (Cups and Coins/Batons and Swords)
> SLOW /FAST (Cups and Coins/Batons and Swords)

What I'm doing here is point to metaphors we live by, that is to say, symbolic representations of verbal communication, space, time, distance, and speed. Because we operate with nothing but the figurative and the symbolic, rules and conventions, there's no such thing as a cartomancy system that has answers for you through a set method that rules. Method rules nothing. You do. There's no such fixed thing as, 'if it's black, it's bad'. No, it's not. Not if you're a general in the army.

QUESTION: Will I win the war? This is a warrior asking.

CARDS: Ace of Spades plus 10 Spades.

ANSWER: Rejoice. You win the war.

Context and common sense determine the answer, not a book of random meanings on the internet. You can use lists of symbolic ideas instrumentally for inspiration, but you can never use them to create an original and coherent narrative that you own. Let me make this explicit point: when you read cards in line for a coherent narrative or a specific aim that actually goes somewhere, something a lot of people find strenuous, what you do is actually activate this type of vocabulary, rather than the one that prioritizes lists of meanings devoid of the dynamic power of connecting. Insofar as meaning is always relational, it makes little sense to upgrade it to a fixed status. There is no such thing as 'this means that'. There's only, 'this means that at this point in time because there's a context that prompts it.' As they say, 'context is king.'

Do you have a question? A well thought out and eloquently formulated question? Congratulations. You got the key to half the answer. You don't have a question? No worries. You can let the cards themselves formulate a question for you. But you *need* a question. You don't get off the hook, if divination is what you want to practice. To an extent, the critique against navel gazing through psychologizing the self with the cards is justified, that is to say, when it points to how this process goes nowhere, when what we do is merely find excuses for our desires to identify with this or that archetype or super power. You can cast a card a day for inspiration, 'here's the Emperor, I can also be like the Emperor,' but would this practice qualify as divining? 'A daily' is using the card as a window towards mirrors that can reflect a new desired identity. Fair enough. But, again, if divination is what you want to do, I'd insist: you *need* a question. Some would also insist, often without an argument, that you *can* experience the oracular without a question. I say you can't. Imagine Oedipus showing up to consult the oracle at Delphi. You think he had no question? Think again.

A CONCRETE EXAMPLE OF NO QUESTION VS. QUESTION

I'll read below a classical square of 13 cards from the French tradition, where the first card down either emphasizes the significator, or is about the theme of the reading when no question is asked. In my case here, and unlike my regular practice, I let the first card determine the theme. The card at the bottom is the surprise. I always read this as a full stop or as a punch line to the narrative that I come up with.

I won't unpack the reading, as I normally do in the context of teaching a class, but rather just go for it, with complete disregard for standard symbolic meanings. Obviously I'm well-aware of the fact that metaphors are also 'meanings' since they are part of linguistic conventions, but what I'm interested in here is more what *we* do with words, rather than what words do *with* us. Therefore, the only thing that interests me is sticking to the commonsensical knowledge of what I can logically infer is the function of each suit: *to drink with the cups, to transact with money, to build with batons, and to stab with the swords.*

In this book you will hear this mantra repeatedly. This is the only principle of the strategy of reading the cards, as it also relates to the idea of either scarcity (1, or a little) or plenitude (10, or a lot).

79

I
LLBATELEVR

ROYNE·DESPEE·

IIII
IIII

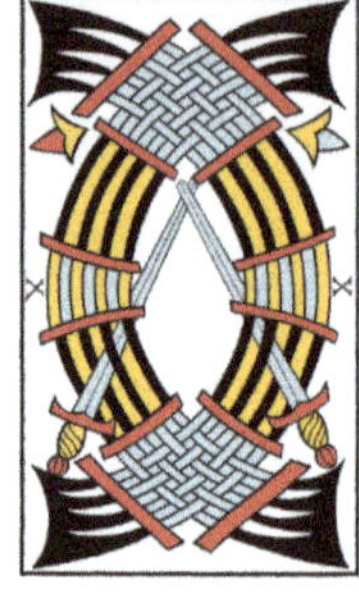
X
X

CHEVALIERDECOVPES

LAROVEDEEORTVNE

VII
I·N
LECHARIOT

V
V

VALETDEBASTONS

X
X

Let's see what the Magician, the first card down here, has to say. The premise for my reading takes point of departure in what I can presume a Magician does. As we're with a trump card here, we look at function: the Magician performs the function of demonstrating his skill at entertaining with the purpose of earning some money. This will be the theme of my reading. Had the Ace of Swords been my first card, I would have said that the theme would be utter sharpness and cutting through whatever the other cards would show is the case.

Let's look at how we can proceed with having nothing in the head other than a sense of how we can manipulate with the temporal and spatial metaphors, as they lend themselves to the idea of connection (pips) in relation to function (trumps and court cards). All in one line. You can be the judge of the extent to which this method of reading the pip cards makes sense, or is useful. I myself like it a lot, simply because it never wastes my time.

THE RELUCTANT MAGICIAN

The Magician would rather not play with any sharp object (AS) in order to gain money (7D), but he can't run from the Queen of Swords who makes sure to remind him of how his painful indifference towards lovely offerings (4S, 10S, KC) leaves everything up to Fortune that favours even the bold ones (Charioteer), who can never get enough of travelling to big cities (AC), in spite of the pain (5S) induced by having to dismount and exercise with a stick, in order to make the jetlag go away, or to simply convince.

Ah, work! So much work for so little money. Thirteen cards and only one related to money... Why so much pressure? Who likes to work so much? Not the Magician. It's clear that this one here is not very efficient. He starts out with a small stick between his fingers that's easy to manipulate, and ends up with a big one that he'll have trouble handling for the purpose of make-believe.

Granted, Houdini could make an entire city disappear, but insofar as our surprise card here is one of a heavy load, not one that suggests an elegant *poof,* we cannot infer that our Magician, who is not really into money, is of the same calibre as the most famous sleight-of-hand mentalists of the world.

In this short narrative, we have thus seen how flow can be created by just looking at the interplay between the function of the trump cards, the pips and the courts. As there's symmetry in play at the formal level of this layout of cards, with the Magician beginning the story and the Page of Batons finishing it, we can also consider the latter as a 'lesser' version of the Magician. Why? Because of rhyme, not because of aspect. I've already suggested this rhyme. It's the one between the small stick in the Magician's hand and the big stick in the Page's hand. Without this rhyme, we'd have to think of the Page as someone other than the Magician, someone who participates in the events that the Magician sets in motion.

As you will see later in the chapter on the court cards, I prefer it that the courts in a reading are given the status of 'other people', rather than see them as variations or aspects of the main significator. But the reason why I want to introduce the idea of rhyme – an idea that comes from studies in poetry and poetics, psychoanalysis and dream interpretation, is because rhyme is very much also a connecting trope. For instance, a more thorough break-down of the rhyming elements in our cards here would further disclose how the Magician is connected or not, to his own sense of competence and where it's going, in terms of developing it. There's a rhyming scheme here between three upstanding swords and three wheels. One sword for each wheel. That's worse than having a stick in your wheel.

So what can we infer? That this Magician is rolling with it in a smooth way? Hardly. Perhaps now we can see why he's so eager for sticks. But will sticks be of use, if rolling is what he wants? Not really. What can we then further infer? Maybe the idea that the Magician would be better off turning around and listening to the Queen in the picture. If she critiques his mental dribbling, poking at his golden nuggets, perhaps there's a reason. What would happen if he didn't feel so threatened? Perhaps he wouldn't end up facing a wall of batons...

My theory is that the pip cards create flow in a reading by making us pay attention to how events and their progression are connected and by what means. In this sense the pip cards can act as something other than their visual or symbolic character. They can say things like this: 'however magically you try, if you don't know the value of sharpness as it relates to timing, you'll find that your effort is nothing but an exercise in displaying power by proxy.' This is another way of putting into words what I see is happening in the thirteen cards above.

Now, if I were to approach this tableau from the perspective of a question, my reading would reflect that focus. If my question was, 'will the plumber be able to fix my kitchen pipes?' I might go like this, reading the cards in three snappy lines: the Magician plumber is resourceful, but he can't identify on his own where the troublesome orifices in the pipes are. He needs the Queen of Swords to tell him where the leak is (first row of cards). It looks like there's a problem in two places, where the water gathers, first a medium size issue and then there's a whole lot punctures allowing the water to flow in a cycle (second row of cards). The Magician has a moment of eureka, 'yay, it's in the bag!' He wants to triumph, but upon closer inspection, he realizes that he needs to call in his apprentice (third row of cards).

So, will the plumber fix the pipes? Not immediately. There's too much work involved. Is the Queen interested in seducing him instead, since the pipes are almost beyond repair? At least there could be that… Not this queen. Anyone making a pass at her will have the pleasure of seeing their guts spill over in the seductive cup, a cup of blood. As for her own seducing, sure, if the Magician were a serious man.

End of story.

Think of what creates coherence in your narrative, cohesive markers, words such as 'however', 'and', 'but', 'consequently,' 'furthermore', 'full stop.' Now think of how your pip cards can represent such words. Try it. I bet your readings will fly, as I also bet that you won't be able anymore to locate your fear of the pip cards, even if you tried. With this in mind, let's move on to hearing what the court cards have to say, before we'll plunge right into the more seductive and dancing power of the pips.

A Short Theory of the Court Cards

ONE OF THE QUESTIONS that I often get in teaching cartomancy pertains to how we distinguish between the court cards. Who is who on the table, when the court cards show up? I read the cards according to the function that I see each card embodies, whether I look at trumps, pip cards, or the court cards. The suits are stylized ideas of our natural laws, as these interact with our way of coping with them.

— The wind is too strong? Well, build a house.

— With what?

— How about some trees?

BATONS

Can we think of trees, in their stylized form as batons on the cards, as having an association to the concept of building, chopping wood and all that Zen-like attitude towards routine work that would be a good idea for us all to have, lest we should succumb to too much pressure. Indeed, we *can* think of the primary meaning of batons as 'work'.

What else do we know of trees? They tend to grow tall in the air. The wind has a funny sound through the trees and their crowns.

— Would it make sense to associate the trees with air, then?

— I should think so.

What else? Trees have an interesting structure in their bark. Sometimes we can think of it as heavy skin. Rough. Unpolished. The bark smells. It smells of the woods and the natural world. Sometimes animals take a pee on the trees, and then some funny looking weeds, both poisonous and not, grow by the roots. Hmm, I wonder what it all means. Very Saturnian.

If we gather the dead branches out in the woods, we can make a mighty fire with them. That is, after we build that luxury log house we dream about, the one that protects us from the strong western winds, or from the hustle and bustle of the city, its merchants and their transactions enabled by weirdly looking processed golden coins that tend to have the face of some schmuck leader or other imprinted on them. Well, not real gold nowadays, as folks down history have long since given up on the necessity to have real gold passing through their hands whenever they need to trade shit for shine.

This wise decision was, of course, mediated by the merchants of the world, the sanguine folks, very good at rhetoric, and very good at convincing the wood people of the benefits of working for the government. After all, when you're done with your own log house, maybe you can build ten or a hundred more just like it. All it requires is hard work. But you won't mind it, really, as what you're good at is in fact exactly that, chopping wood — whether for your own private use or for the public condo. Who cares? You get paid, and work exhilarates you.

— Is the King of Batons a King of work, then?

— Why, yes he is.

What else do we know of the King of Batons, other than the fact that he smells, he works like a maniac and demands the same? He plans a lot – all that wood needs counting – he builds connections, and he's good at figuring out which stick fits what hole. That's quite enough already. Essentially, however, all we need to do is think this: the suit of Batons equals a whole lot of wood.

COINS

Whoever is in charge of the coins, and now virtual banking transactions, belongs to the group of very smart folks. Their brains are irrigated by blood in an almost mystical way. Well, so it goes with all the trickster gods. If they're good at anything, that'd be commerce and how to make others work for them. Yep. You gotta have a lot of brain power to convince the wood folks to work for you. And then for what exactly? For losing the very thing that feeds their need for work. How many more forests must go down? Too many. The result? A cold and dry temperament. The wood folks will get depressed – 'melancholic' they used to call it – and will soon be in need of making a new transaction: more work in exchange for a soul.

If the coins type of folk, the Mercurial type, will not be able to provide the service, they will be sure to direct the wood folks to a professional. They are after all masters of fixing ambivalence. They know everything about crossroads, whether asphalt or clay. The coin folks are *wired*.

The water people are the phlegmatics of the world.

— What's that?

— Well, that is desire with a capital D.

Here comes Venus, the Goddess of Love and Money. We all want that, but some want that really badly. They will pray to the moon and back for it. Just think of what we do with water in its stylized form as we find it on the cards in the form of cups filled with liquid, or as hearts. With cups we make a toast, invite friends for a nice ritual of libation, and then watch how everybody will get their tongues untied, giving way to a whole lot of repressed emotions and desires, disclosing also just what a mighty power the power of insatiable desire is.

If the wood folks come to the water folks, the water folks will know how to show sympathy. On rare occasion they will show compassion, Jupiter style, but sympathy is more frequent. After all, since the water folks crave stuff all the time, and they are *the* masters at craving, there's only so much empathy they can display. But they will be able to hear the pulse in your veins, pumping through your heart. This pulse is close to what the water folks are good at identifying: circulation. Any flow of blood is their specialty.

SWORDS

Spilling blood. That's the domain of the choleric folks, the Mars folks, the warriors, the ones who are good with a sword in their hands. They have one mantra only, which they repeat incessantly: 'Off with their heads.'

When they're done with all that chopping of heads, guess what, some digging is necessary. Where do you suppose that all those spades represented on playing cards come from? Digging the earth. Swords and death. Do you see the connection? The two malefics, Mars and Saturn. You don't want to go against them. Their presence in any layout spells out *trouble*.

Imagine to live in this paradox: in order to know the coldness of the earth, you need to have a very hot head, blinding your actions. *En garde!*, the Solar fixated French cloak and dagger folks used to shout all the time in those noble days of chivalric retribution, using their hottest passion and their coldest head, thus inverting the order of things: hot head and cold passion. But who cares, as long as somebody dies. Exhilarating. If the choleric swordsmen play their cards right, they might even get either the wood folks to dig the graves for the dead, or the water folks to officiate the burial, or more likely to shed some tears on behalf of the community. Where do you think that all those traditions of lamentation come from? Keening, anyone? The Irish are very good at it. Not to mention the Romanians. 'Who's going to die?' is *the* question here.

I don't know about you, but I have participated in many funerals, including those of my parents where I've witnessed the following: the wood folks provided the coffins and the external planning of what to do with the dead corpse, how to dress it and all that. Work. The water folks provided the libation and the tears. Family comforting. The coin folks took our money and promised to facilitate help in case of a nervous breakdown. Fast messengers. The earth folks dug the graves with their spades, and nailed the coffins. Friend or foe? We all sit at the table together, eating or stabbing each other if the drinks go to our heads. We sit together in church, or by somebody's grave. We comfort each other, or slander each other. We love each other, or kill each other.

The suits represent the four universal types we all recognize from our walks of life. Some are lumpers, some are splitters. The court cards leading the numbers are all faithful representatives of their kingdoms.

What does a King do? Sit on it, sit on his achievements. A King is above having to prove himself, to consolidate stuff, to make transactions. He delegates. He has others do these things for him. Therefore he embodies a symbol of power in its static manifestation. If Cups, man of love; if Batons, man of work; if Coins, man of money; if Swords, man of war.

The Knight is an emblem of consolidating the King's business in an active way. He's into developing. The difference between a symbol of power and an emblem of development is one of rank. The Knight acts on behalf of, whereas the King is at the top, commanding and controlling power.

The Queens as the creators of the world fulfill their function of being guardians of sacred knowledge, and hence of truth. They embody a different kind of power that's aligned with how we see with the logical eyes and how we see with the so-called illogical eyes — this latter idea, especially as seen from the perspective of culture.

Pages are agents at the mercy of others. They are sons and daughters, messengers, or apprentices. Their presence in a string of cards, especially if the string consists of the highest rank court cards, can indicate the thoughts or emotions of these higher powers. The Page of Cups can be an emotional extension of what the Queen of Cups is thinking about, or what she intends to act towards. They can also be seen as stages towards the manifestation of the mighty power that a King possesses.

If the King of Swords doubts as to whether he must engage and go to war or not, the presence of the Page of Swords in the sequence of cards will most likely confirm this ambivalence, the Page of Swords being a nasty little thing, always intent on splitting relations, rather than finishing them off the honorable way, in a duel, or by actually going to war.

The Page of Coins aspires to make money, but he lacks the cunningness of the King of Coins. At the other pole, the Page of Cups is always sweet and floundering, encouraging his single mother to find a husband for herself. Oh, the sympathy that can turn nasty, if the Queen is too impressionable herself, and unable to discern what the truth is.

I see the idea that the Queen equals truth as related to the way we make a distinction between the public and the private spheres. At least that's my conclusion after reflecting on the cunning folk cartomancy, often referenced by others in various books and online resources, yet without full explanations as to why we equate a court card with a certain idea (see, for instance, a favorite of mine, Dawn Jackson's *hedgewytch* method that, although logically wonderful and sound, often falls short of examining the root of the logical thread behind why we say what we say).

This is fair enough, as the best way to go about it is to think for yourself. Let us assume, then, that since a queen is not considered 'a man of action' she may sit on the domain of thought, thus approving of our attitude of thinking for ourselves. Consequently, after I was done with my own share of thinking about it, here is what I have arrived at: traditionally men have occupied the public sphere – well, they still do – and women the private sphere.

Where is it more likely to find the truth? Obviously not in the public sphere where politicians set the agenda. The truth is the closest to us, our private place, our soul. Who has access to this? Women. That's my reasoning. I haven't seen others talk about it in this specific way, though it is likely that you can stumble over similar, albeit much more abstract notions.

In books about esoteric tarot people refer to the court cards as having to do with an expression of the 'within and without' dichotomy, or indeed as following the hermetic axiom: 'as above, so below' (see for ex. Marcus Katz's work). In other tarot books that have a psychological bent, you'll come across the court cards as described in terms of their helping or non-supportive attitude (from counselors to abusers, critics, victims, champions, and so on; see Kate Warwick Smith's work).

FUNCTIONS

As far as I'm concerned, the court cards qualify to *perform a function* all according to the suit they embody and the context of the question. Whether the King of Swords is a bad magician today and a good magistrate tomorrow will be something we can determine according to how we see the essential qualities of the suit of swords in alignment with the context of the question. Furthermore, the distance between action and truth, the public sphere and the private sphere, and men and women is also determined by the surrounding cards. If your question is about your need to know some truth, or it has an investigative character, then the presence of the Queen will tell you what you need to focus on. If the Swords, the truth is distorted; if the Cups the truth flows. The other suits give you a 'maybe'. It's the question and the context that give you the answer to when the Queen acts as an emblem of truth or not. What is the question, exactly?

If the question is one about how to handle the truth, then the presence of the Queen of Swords alongside the King of Cups suggests difficulty in admitting to suffering from blind spots. The Page of Swords alongside the Queen of Swords suggests intentional lying, where the Page modifies the Queen's thoughts or intent for the worse. The Knight of Batons can be a real estate agent when in the presence of the King of Coins, and so on.

Beyond cultural pre-conditioning, when we have to determine who all these court people are, populating our spreads, we can remind ourselves that we can also see with something other and more than our cognitive capacity to decode, interpret, and make aesthetic evaluations or judgments.

We can see how, following the suits, we are more prone to becoming obsessed with money than with work, and committing a crime of passion than passionately going to war. The reason for this is related to the closeness of the four stylized ideas in the cards of love, money, work, and war to our own concerns.

Coins make us sweaty and hot. The heart can beat fast and rush us into action. Work schemes won't excite us nearly as much as money schemes, and war hardly ever wins in the affairs of the heart – the head may fall, the heart, never. Swords and batons are long, and we hold them at arm's length. We hold coins in our palms, and the blood in our veins keeps us alive. What is our most immediate need? Shelter and love. Money buys us the house and the bedroom. We only need to go to war, or compete, if the neighbor has her eyes on our property.

THE SELF AND THE OTHER

Court cards always represent other people. They hardly ever represent 'aspects' of ourselves, not even when we try to stretch our esoteric politeness. Court cards as aspects of us are pretty useless, and in mundane questions they never work. Telling someone who gets the Queen of Cups and the Queen of Coins side by side that this indicates how she can sometimes be full of love and other times full of brains will hit a nerve, for sure. But how specific is that? Aren't we all like that? Aren't we sometimes loving and sometimes innovative? Generalities never move anyone. Think in specific terms beyond the cliché.

The best is to go old school, and always pick a significator before laying out any larger spread of cards. The significator must be aligned first with the profession of the person asking the question, and then, following tradition, with the physical traits. Traditionally, a blondish, a red head, or a woman with white hair, is represented by the Queen of Coins. If she's a professor, or manages the bank, you're set. I start with this latter attribution.

The Queen of Cups is a mother, or a woman working in healthcare. She also tends to be totally blond – go figure... The Queen of Batons knows her business, and handles practical matters with mastery. She is an enterprising brunette. The Queen of Spades is the darkest in complexion, and works as a judge or a bad witch – the question decides who is who.

The King of Batons is a manager or boss, of dark complexion, and the King of Cups a father, a counsellor, or a priest, a blond man. The King of Swords is a magistrate, a policeman, George Clooney in *Ocean's Eleven*, or a mentalist. Usually he is the darkest in complexion. The King of Coins is a financial tycoon, freckled or reddish blond towards olive complexion.

The Knight follows suit regarding profession and physical traits, and acts as a delegate. If the King is a general, the Knight is his soldier (Swords). If the King is a bank director, the Knight speculates on Wall Street (Coins). If the King is a cardiologist, the Knight is a seducer (Cups). If the King is a developer, the Knight is a forest ranger (Batons).

Pages study or deliver messages (Coins), meddle in others' affairs without concern (Swords), work for a herbalist (Batons), or daydream (Cups). There's hardly any ambiguity as to who does what and for what purpose. Because of this purpose, the court cards give us a sense of direction. In their presence we're not in any situation that makes us doubt: 'maybe this is also an aspect of you immolating yourself.' Yeah, right…

'If you give me that money you sit on,' the Queen of Coins says to her husband, 'I'll make sure to invest it. Others will follow my example, and before you know it, we can even start a school. How about I teach cartomancy students the art of having their palms crossed with silver? Okay, make that *gold…*'

Trumps, Courts, & Pips in Tableaus

L ET'S LOOK BRIEFLY at a couple of examples: the first is the classical square of 9 cards. This example comes from a reading for a woman writer whose field is Western esotericism and occultism. No, it's not me, but I relate. I picked the Queen of Diamonds as her significator. I did not put her aside, but left her in the pack.

Generally, if the significator shows up in the spread, it will indicate that the querent will take an active part in the dynamics of what is being asked about. If not, then we can see it as a sign that the querent will be impacted on by factors that are more external to her concern. On special occasion, there's also the possibility that, although the significator remains hidden in the pack, another card among the courts can 'insist' on representing the querent. If you think this is the case, then make sure to look very carefully at all the cards on the table, to ensure that you have just cause for assigning agency to a court card that's not already the pre-selected representative of your querent. You *want* to do this, because otherwise there would be no reason why you should have a method to begin with, one that carefully distributes the active powers among the players on your table.

Here is the woman's question: 'what exactly characterizes the people I write for, and how can I best serve them? How do I develop a stronger sense of belonging?'

VALET DE BASTONS

LE·PAPE

LA·PAPESSE

In this 9-card tableau we got only one court card. This is not so surprising, given the nature of the question to identify the traits of the folks the querent wishes to belong to and serve. The court cards tend to pop more frequently in questions about family or relationships at work.

I picked this example, however, even though it only features one court card here, the Page of Batons, because I found that it participated in giving a very literal answer. As the significator, the Queen of Coins, didn't show up in the spread, we can infer that this is due to her having some doubts, indeed, as to where her writing belongs. But it's clear that her skills belong with the spiritual folks. I say this for two reasons:

First, by the special rule that I was talking about earlier, we could see the Popess here, the woman of the book facing the Pope, as a representative of the querent, at least as far as the distribution of agency according to the function in context goes. There's a mirroring here at the situational level, where we can say that the woman of the book asking a question about the book gets to see a woman of the book on the table. 'This must be her,' we can assume, though it's best to verify all our assumptions before we pass final judgment on who is doing what to whom. Let's see if this assumption holds here too.

Second, the cards themselves verify the context: the woman querent writes about esoteric matters, and we get to see the clergy on the table. I wouldn't say that there's relatability here, as I find 'relatability' a fraught concept, but I'd say that we're definitely here with some form of belonging. But what kind?

More immediately, we observe that the center card is the Pope, flanked to the left by the Page of Batons, handling a rough staff, and the Popess, indeed, handling a book. The Page here is simply the altar boy, who is also out in the yard fixing things. The cards in the middle spell it out quite clearly that the querent's folk is church folk, or ritualists.

What we can note is that we have quite a preponderance of coins and cups over batons and swords. Swords are not even represented at all. We're thus with the suits close to us, giving us access to what we hold in our hands in a more intimate way, cups and coins, rather than the distant swords and batons.

If we were to describe the people our querent is interested in writing for and about, we'd say the following: they have money problems, but know the way of the heart and how to have a good time (7 Coins, 6 Cups, 3 Cups).

As we're with the coins here, representing mental power within the context of the church and ritual, we can impose a spiritual reading on the card of the 7 Coins as it relates to div-ination and fortunetelling, clairvoyance and mystical vision. Basically, if you're 'mental' in the context of the church, that means that you're a mystic of sorts.

In a magical setting, the cards marked as number 7 are the only cards that can change status, from indicating trouble, in a mundane situation, to suggesting shapeshifting; vision if coins, practical and talismanic magic if batons, mysticism and gnosis if cups, and 'black' magic, if swords.

At the core of this tribe is a spiritual leader, attended by his apprentice, and a wise woman (Page of Batons, Pope, Popess). The community may struggle with money, but when the folks here get their hands on it, they spend it all on themselves, and then take a ride on the flying carpet towards the One love (5 Coins, Ace of Coins, Ace of Cups). These folks are good at casting circles, creating some good sigils, and making lavish

offerings in the form of libations, judging by the looks of the
Ace of Coins and the Ace of Cups.

If ever a spiritual community is led by the motto: 'love is all
you need', we get a confirmation of it here. The Page's work
consists of swinging his baton between visions and relics. With
lots of vigor. Money goes into setting up altars that look good
and smell good, or some other type of ritual jewelry that spiritual folks like to adorn themselves with (7 Coins, Page of Batons, 5 Coins). The Pope leads the way and delivers messages
of roundness: 'God bless everyone, and don't fall off the magic
carpet. Have another ritual drink' (6 Cups, Pope, Ace of Coins;
6s are for travel). Everyone enjoys the party under the watchful
eye of the High Priestess, who makes sure that the Holy Grail
is filled to the brim with the good stuff (3 Cups, Popess, Ace of
Cups).

This tribe is into love and visions, money magic, and wisdom. Who wouldn't want to belong here? A good message for
our Queen of Diamonds, the querent, who was already on this
path, having written some short stories that had magic as a
topic. But she wanted to know how she could make herself
more visible to this tribe, especially upon observing that her
presence was missing from this party. Not seeing her significator on the table, other than through the projection that the
Popess *could* be her, as this *was* her desired identity, she was
concerned that she wrote for people who didn't really see her,
while nonetheless consuming her offerings. So the trouble
here was that the querent saw herself as both represented
through her nature and not represented through recognition.

I turned up the bottom card from the cut deck. It disclosed
the 7 Cups.

'More love,' I said. Make an offering, and stand out. You belong already. The 7 Cups is a card of spirituality, so start contributing to filling that big chalice in the middle with your own libations. It will be appreciated.' But then I added the note that, traditionally, whenever the Popess shows up in the layout, she has a relation to the querent, if not representing the querent directly, then in an implicit way.

Again, the link here between the Popess and her book and the Queen of Coins and her book was more direct, given the writing profession. Thus, beyond mere assumption, we have reason to go with the literally obvious, including the pun: as the Popess deals with books, she not only mirrors, but also embodies what the Queen of Coins does: thinks a lot, and reads and writes.

As you can see, then, although we didn't have any reason to wonder about agency here, or fret about the question of who is who, we could read the single court card in this tableau precisely according to the function that it performs: a young man participating in making the spiritual community magical, and also giving a direct message to the querent about the more nuanced aspects of the community of people she is serving, ritual being one of their primary concerns.

My advice was to write more intricately about all aspects of 'church' life, and suggest what talismanic value love has for organized spirituality.

∞

The second example features a line of 5 cards, for which I picked no significator in advance. A man wanted to know: 'what is our common goal in our family?'

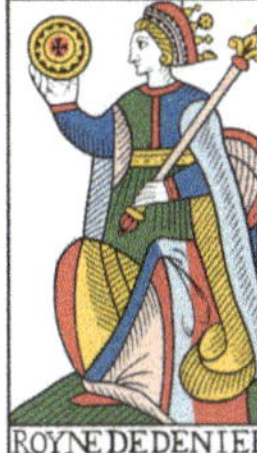

Following the direction of the gazes in this spread we notice the following: the goal is money. It starts with a financial-like meeting presided over by the woman of money, the Queen of Coins, who brings her own contribution to it. A loving young man, the Page of Cups, follows this woman (not his blood mother, as the querent also validates), and brings his emotions to the table. The Magician watches the parade, and follows the Page of Cups. He is probably also thinking: can I make more money? The Queen is closer to the money than the Magician, so money is more important to her than it is to him. He is gazing towards money from some distance, but it looks like he enjoys more the idea that he can just make money happen out of the blue. That's what a Magician does, after all.

The last card in this line indicates a tension. Although the common goal seems to be chasing after money, the Magician is not on the same page as the Queen and the Page. He even seems to be wondering: what's this fascination with money that the Queen mirrors and the Page desires?

The card of Force shows a woman trying to tame an animal. A force seems to pull the Magician away from the monetary goal, enticing him to recalibrate his focus on something wilder and more essential than the culture of money. As he is not aware of this force – he's not looking towards what else is there – it is no wonder that he ends up seeking the service of a fortuneteller, who can help him sort out the family circus. A good thing we're here to serve.

A Community of Agents

The court cards are agents helping us or blocking us from achieving what we want. They counsel us, sell us down the river, talk behind our backs, or stab us. They are mortals who act in their own right, just like we do. A good reading of the court cards will take into consideration the dynamics of the interrelation between ourselves and others, our contexts and platform for action and those of others. Sometimes we mirror ourselves in what the courts do, but these agents are never us.

We come into the world, we live, and we die. While quite alone on our life path, we encounter others who tell us their stories. This is the function of the court cards: to tell us a story that teaches us something about ourselves, how to live and die better, how to better breathe the air we share, and how to think of our own role and place on this planet. If we're still confused, we can call in the trumps, or let the numbers speak what there is to speak in that beautiful and abstract manner that only numbers are capable of. In our perception of love and hate, love is always like an unreliable elastic. We can die equally well — and beautifully, some Romantics might say — if we stretch it to 10, or not at all. Too much love or too much hate can put a stop to breathing. The same goes for the absence of either of these strong emotions. No love can make your soul wither. No hatred makes your life shallow. What *can* you do, if you don't hate your competition at least a little bit? Only Zen masters can escape their emotional elastic of identifications…

'What do you want from me?' people who don't know what to do with you ask, especially when you yourself don't know what to do with yourself. 'Nothing,' you can say. 'Everything is settled already. As long as there's wine, there's always someone to drink it with. Death minds her own business.' The subtle burst here is the implicit in the cards: the chopped heads of 'nothing' are the two cups rising…

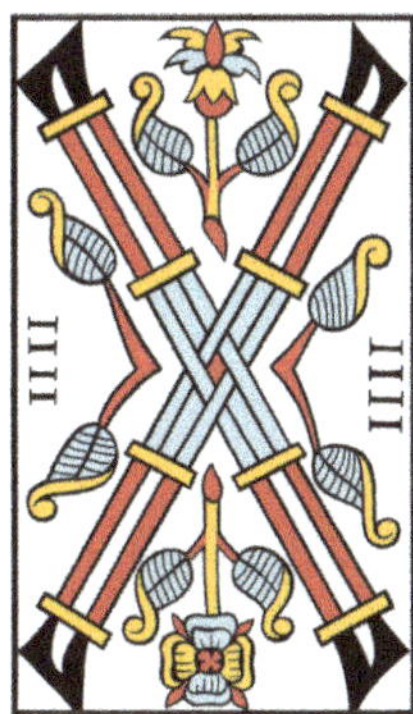

In the next chapter we're going to look at the ways in which numbers can be brought closer to our mundane experiences, while retaining their infinite, mathematical potential.

The Elastic as a Method

ONE OF THE POINTS I STRESS in all my cartomancy teachings is the idea of reading by stretching our internal elastic of perception. As soon as we lay down some cards, after the initial preliminary observations that I urge the students to make, what we engage with is answering questions about the elasticity of a story put on our table, or the situation and its context: how far is this story stretched? Where is the limit of this stretching? Is there any stretching at all? Can I stretch it some more? If I stretch it and it bursts, then what?

The best way to demonstrate what exactly constitutes the power of the court and pip cards is by thinking of the function of connecting that they perform. Whereas the trump cards operate with grand concepts, the court cards mediate between them, letting us see how these concepts unfold. The pip cards' function in this respect is to point to what punctuates such unfolding. They are our markers for coherence and cohesion.

One of my favorite examples of such punctuation, not only as a stylistics sign, but also as a structure sign is the 10 Cups. Traditionally everyone wants to link the 10 cups depicted on the card with love and the epitome of sentimental attachment. I prefer to see this card as a full stop to emotional content (a stylistic sign), and as a context marker: 'enough of this already!' (a structural sign).

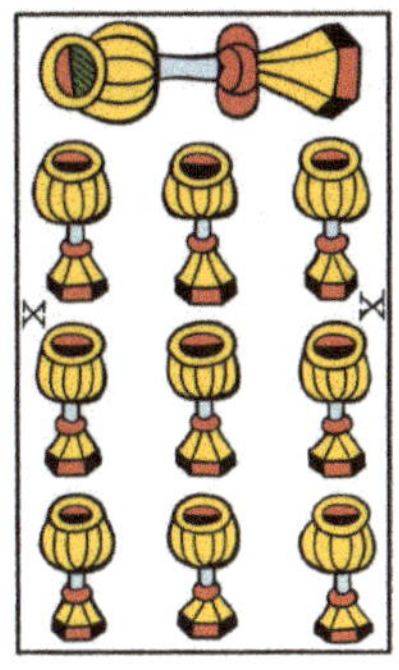

Taken out of context, the 10 Cups still speaks for *a* context, as most tend to think in numerical terms: 10 cups of love sounds better than 2, even when there's the possibility for intimate toasting. Definitely the 10 cups tell us that love is here to stay. Or not. Visually, it's hard to disconnect the one large cup at the top from the others neatly arranged, and assign it positive value. A tilted cup spells out spillage. This party is over. Too much is too much. How about that marriage that went all the way in the vows, and then, splash? Oh, but the *feels*. Let's think of another example:

We're looking here at the Fool, 10 Batons, and Ace of Swords. If we go the traditional way, we can say this: 'the Fool is free. He has great ideas, and his mind is as sharp as an axe.' Fair enough. But how about this idea? If the Fool hits a wall of 10 Batons, perhaps we can say that he's lucky not to end up impaling himself. Those 10 batons will sure put up a lot of resistance. Knowing how fortune favors the fools, we may speculate that this one here may be lucky enough to dodge the danger. Unawares, he hits the wall that protects him.

The context determines which reading is more valid. Sometimes you read for the plot, and other times for pleasure. You can go with lists of meanings, until you get tired of them. Lists of meanings *do not* create context, nor do they address specific points of contexts, but they *can* be instrumentally instructive. For this reason lists are fascinating, and for the most part,

when we actually remember where the associations come from, they can even be a lot of fun. For your own education, you can even learn to go by the alphabet where single cards are concerned. Try creating yours. When I think *lists,* however, I first think: to what extent does this association make sense? Let's take the queen of Cups as an example of going *ad hoc* by the alpahbet:

A   actress, adulteress, affection, art, admiration, alms
B   banquet, beauty parlor, bed, bonnet, breasts, bliss
C   cake, carpets, caresses, cats, cheers, consent, cure
D   desire, diabetes, disgrace, drama, dolls, dresses
E   ease, elegance, emeralds, elite, eloping, estrogen
F   fancy, fashion, feminism, fertility, finery, forgiving, fun
G   game, glamor, girls, gluttony, gratitude, grace, garden
H   heart, hair, handicraft, hat, happy, honeymoon, hotel
I   indolence, incest, intimacy, impregnation, invitation
J   jewelry, joy, jokes, jelly, juvenile, jolly, jubilant
Z   zest

You get the picture. Now, how do you know that you'll want more from your cards than a list of keywords that I can ask you to memorize, or you have jotted down in your shadow book of magic, along with others you have learnt by heart? You will know that the time has arrived for more, when you realize that you actually want to speak *from* the heart, not *by* heart. If you tried already, however, to tell people that you got tired of lists, and that you want to speak this visual language in your own words, then I bet you've met resistance. How dare you don't bow to the ones that came before you, be just like them!

Refusing to speak the language of authority is a sign of insolence, seen from the authority's point of view. But what *is* this language of authority? Just look at the LWB ('Little White Book') accompanying any deck you have. Here's one from my deck, *Tarot Maddonni* by Grimaud (1981):

> If we examine the old Tarot de Marseille we perceive that Mademoiselle Maddonni has not diverged from it very much, since each card here kept the traditional precision with regard to meaning and symbolism. In order to read the cards with greater insight, you must try to memorize the forty odd 'key words' that are suggested for each arcana and each suit of cards. When you have learnt these key words by heart, you will be able to assess them easily after consulting the chapter MEANING OF THE CARDS.

Let's just say that my whole work with the Tarot is to get people to speak in their own voice, according to an assessment of the question and what the context is all about. Each card is built around a commonsensical truth and thus holds a principal essence that's not symbolic or archetypal. The point is that memorizing lists of meanings will not give you a sense of the interplay between rulership and timing — who does what to whom and when — as it also relates to the idea of flow and dominion. The court cards sit on it, dominantly. The number cards ensure that there's flow in the sitting on it. Even when blockage is experienced, insofar as the number cards show you how strong or how weak the blockage is, they give you an opportunity to do something about it.

The pip cards thus give us insight into the degree of formality and conventionality that we find at societal and structural level against the spontaneity of everyday life. The pip cards are thus mirrors of opposites: tension and release; connection and disconnection; surface and depth; mobility and fixity. The pip cards give us something to think about when we reflect on the elastic of social structures.

I've stated on a number of occasions that when it comes to tracing the common-sense aspect of cartomancy, or the cunning-folk nerve in cartomancy, what we observe is the following: it's all about rulership and timing. Who rules over what and whom? When does it happen, and how does it happen? The court cards are about *agency:* people influencing other people. The pip cards are about *modifications:* is the rulership good or bad, serious, devoted, superficial, cunning, lousy, lazy, hypocritical, pathetic, exalted, idealistic, advanced, primitive, honorable, or indifferent? Is the timing and momentum for decisions and directives right, or is it vexing and vacillating?

The pip cards emphasize seasons, speed, flow, and distance. Everything we have to say about that is subsumed by a set of metaphors: winter is slow, and for most people ugly, as you can easily end up with broken bones. Summer seems far away in relation to it. In winter all is gloomy and the opposite of optimism. This is already a visual language we can relate to.

Things are hot or cold, far and near, up or down, high or low, few or many. Many cups of wine will get you drunk. Shedding one tear is not as bad as shedding a river. We keep going back to this commonsensical observation about the four suits:

Coins are for spring and fire. A fresh idea is born. It's hot. What if we put the face of the Emperor on this forged piece of gold, and call it 'power?' You can get the power if you get the coin. Ooo, can you feel the tension and the excitement? Coins are thus chiselled for exchange and culture. We hold coins in our hands. They denote working with the head. You're a bad merchant if you can't think about transacting strategies. Coins thus relate to mental ability, and represent the nervous system.

Cups are for summer and water. Relax. You had your idea in the morning. It was good. You shared it with others over lunch. Most fell for it. Others not so much. Contain yourself. Don't get emotional about it. Assess your inner flow. Can you take more wine? It can intoxicate your body, making you unable to discern. But you tell the truth, even to your detriment. Or lie. Cups represent the circulatory system.

Batons are for autumn and air. How tall is it, your idea? Does it need harvesting? Batons grow in the air. Tall trees are at arm's length. You exercise with a stick. Batons represent the muscular system.

Swords are for winter and earth. You're done. This idea needs to die to make room for a new one. Swords are forged for protection and conquering. You kill someone, you bury them in the ground. Only bones remain. Swords represent the skeletal system.

There's no such thing as positive and negative cards. When looking at your cards, you can't rigidly say, 'if it's red, it's good, and if it's black, it's bad.' As noted earlier, sometimes the 'bad' cards on the table give you a reason to rejoice. Sometimes winning the war through stabbing others is a very good thing. Try engaging in discoursing on moral philosophy while you're on the battlefield. Your boss would say: 'are you stupid, or something? We need to close this deal, not to debate on legitimizing justice.' You can resist, since you're a righteous softie, but you can also elect to know your place and the situation you're in to begin with. If you don't like the way this company is running things, why are you here? The point is that the context determines the exact value of each card, not a pre-determined meaning assigned to the card according to some general terms of acceptance.

Everything that we can say about ourselves in context would be the same we can say about others. Reading cards is not about memorization and imitation. It's about improvisation and paying attention. The most important questions are questions that address plausibility in action. Is it likely that your querent can marry within a year? Yes, if she's actively seeing people. This is a probable scenario. The cards on the table don't show a set outcome. They point to what is possible.

The court cards mirror the metaphors we use in connection with the way the pip cards create bridges across our ideas. Court cards designate a caste system, pointing to a type of feudalism that's still with us. When somebody dies, you need an undertaker to take care of things and mediate between the grieving family and the office that issues the death certificate. You pay for this service. Somebody builds the coffin, and others dig the grave. You also pay for this service. The family itself weeps, and though you wouldn't think it, you pay for this service too. How about you see these interlinked events as representing the coins, the batons, the swords, and the cups? It's not difficult to see the 'old world' still going strong in its divisions. In fact, it makes perfect sense. We may think we live in a modern world, but everything we get in it is the result of people fulfilling different functions and duties. 'You gotta serve somebody', they say, and they're right. There's no free lunch.

The point I'm trying to hammer on here is that if there's power in the court and pip cards, then it's to be found in this very assessment of how culture moves. Who are the dominant players and how are we positioned vis-à-vis these players? When people come to us and ask us to cast cards for them, we note that the questions they pose spring out of feeling deeply connected to the need to move, to carry on, to acknowledge change and accept it too. Yet the way this connection manifests is often as a disconnect. So there's a constant irony the diviner works against, an irony that you don't find represented in what Little White Books ask you to memorize.

Essentially, although this feeling of a bounded up connection and disconnection may look like the intangible space of 'psychologizing for the self,' the actual reality is that we're dealing with a very real concern with positioning. As most people are caught in the cog of the wheel that's not of fortune, what everyone struggles with is their own power to act. Sometimes you can't act. Sometimes you cry. What is possible in the face of impotence, when many swords and batons block the move forward? How do you think in dynamic ways? We use the full deck of cards when we want an answer to this very question. We look at force and counter force. We practice seeing just what 'key words' emerge out of combinations.

Let's look at this string of paired cards on the opposite page, and suggest some possible scenarios for interpretation.

10 Cups next to 4 Batons suggests a firm resolve to get a grip on yourself. 9 Cups next to 7 Swords is a bad situation. Get more kleenex. 5 Batons next to 8 Coins suggests rolling with your ideas towards financial success. 9 Swords next to 3 Swords can be a sign of relief, or not. Your duty flops. Maybe you're happy that it does. Now there's less of it for you to worry about.

What I'm doing here is simply look at number progression, and tension and release (10 is a lot, 3 not nearly that much). How much is the elastic of unfolding events stretched? Who does the stretching of it? The court cards or the trumps will tell you who is behind the stretching. Numbers will tell you how far.

My aim to create a set of synthesizing ideas out of these pairs relies on applying principles of design, movement, semiotics, and hermeneutics to my reading. This is another way of saying that what I do is look at the interaction between the cards. I don't go, '10 cups means great love' or '4 batons means stability.' Seeing cards as carriers of 'individual personality' can be fascinating in and of itself, but if you want to develop virtuosity in the art of cutting to the bones, then it's not 'meanings' you'll be repeating. Rather, you'll be observing essential and subtle moves. How do you move from the cups to the swords, from the batons to the coins?

Although we have 4 suits in a deck of cards, the movement between them is a simple 2-way understanding of what to keep and what to discard. That's what you want to know.

It is in this observation that I invoke the spirit of martial arts in my cartomancy, as it's all about looking intently at how the cards manifest what you really want to keep and what you want to discard. What do the cards say? Keep the love, or get rid of it? Keep the job or get rid of work? Keep the body workout, or try something new? Keep the boundaries, or take down the fences? The numbers are there to tell you something about the degree of the intensity in your actions, when it comes to what to keep and what to discard.

Let's stretch our elastic some more, or rather, contract it, so that a few essential notes of technical knowledge can emerge. What we want with our elastic is to be on point. That is to say, stretch it neither too much, nor too little, but exactly as much as it's needed. Let's see some contrasts between *list* meanings and *situational* meanings based on these three cards:

Let's take first an example of some keywords according to lists of meanings à la: 'the Queen of Batons means energy; '10 of Coins means a lot of financial resources; 9 of Swords means strife and disappointment.' A possible, coherent interpretation that we can offer here is the following: 'the Queen of Batons manages her money in a disappointing way.'

Now let's take the situational meaning into account, that is to say, when we anchor the possible interpretation of the cards in the *cards in context,* where the context is drawn from assessing how a card signifies: 'the Queen of Batons highly lacks clear and coherent accounting skills.' Or: 'ideas (coins associate with fire and mental constructions; coins are forged in fire and have high symbolic value) are held up in the air (batons associate with trees in the wind) until they flop (swords go with gravity, and digging the earth).

Passing a sentence that's based on situational meaning thus goes through a swift movement regarding the stages of interpretation, from noticing design, to following the trajectory the cards points to, and finally to unpacking the cards' descriptive level so that an evaluative reflection and analysis can lead to a sound conclusion. What I'm doing here is point to the storytelling aspect in divination. Why storytelling? Because what we call 'dynamic relationships' is very much contingent on the successfulness of telling a story of the self in relation. In this telling, we're now past both the dreaded stages of 'psychologizing for the self' and the idealized 'philosophizing on the self.' We're now with rhetoric and rules of composition.

Have you thought about how each culture generates stories about the self, with some placing an almost obsessive emphasis on the individual seen as the center of all things?

You guessed. That would be our Western culture. Let's compare briefly, so we have something to hold ourselves to when we try to understand how the pip cards create value in a reading, and what is being mediated in the process.

Western Europe sees the individual as a moral compass. There's grand mythologizing about the function of MAN understanding his place in the world through his own perception of justice and morality. Greece sees the individual as subject to fate. You're there where you're supposed to be. There's nothing moral or immoral about it. Cosmic justice may have a say in it, though. The Middle East sees the individual as a mirror of the stars. 'As above, so below' starts with Mesopotamian thinking. India sees the individual as one with the infinite absolute. The East sees the individual as part of nature and its flow.

Dominant, at the center of everything? Or part of nature, in the background? When the Greeks said, 'Know thyself', what they meant to say was this: 'know your place.'

The classical view on the maxim 'Know thyself' associates it with the notion of temperance, suggesting a relational process of being in the world that doesn't lead to things blowing up in your face, or making your hands sweat from holding your scepter too tight (see the 10th-century Byzantine encyclopaedia, Suda). To begin with, there is no YOU to blow up, as YOU is part of a web of connections. Whoever holds your possessions is not YOU. Possessions are there by virtue of grace and faith, including all the other intangibles that you wish were concrete. Hence it makes sense that in the classical view we have balance in focus, not the self.

When the courts and the pips are in play, think about how they create a link between you in the web of connections and the awareness you have of your place. In his sense, the power of the pips is on a par with the power of the trumps, insofar as the field for posing grand questions is wide open. My favorite here is this one: how aware are you of your place? Others would call this 'place' their path. I prefer to think of it as my own justice. The Buddhists would say that knowing your place is the realization of truth, which is actually embodied by the realization of NOW. I wrote more extensively about this in *What is Not*, where I delivered the Marseille Tarot à la carte.

In working with the pip cards you can think about how the court cards embody attitudes and how the number cards measure the elasticity of your stretching against the background of this NOW. Therefore the condition for knowing your place is tied with having a sense of timing and momentum and the ability to recognize what events exactly unfold before your eyes.

Here's a fun reading that will give you a concrete sense of what you gain when you see all the cards as connecting events both on the morphological and semantic level, and also at topic level. Let's take this question: 'what is at stake in finding my place in the world?' Ask it for yourselves.

I perform this reading often as part of the program that's called living with oracles, not because they supposedly give me access to life's mysteries, but because they function as a constant reminder of how my 'self' is never more than a thought, a thought that becomes part of verbally negotiating for what is possible and plausible to perform in the world. I may be on 'the path to realization,' but what positions are available to me? My claim here is that much of what we think we're doing when we divine with the cards is actually nothing more than an exercise in naming. Divination and nomenclature go hand in hand. Just think of the people seeking your counsel. How often have you encountered their inability to name their problem? Hence, what they're looking for is for you to name the solution. If both the problem and the solution can be named, then chances are that you can find more words to support you in the vanquishing of the problem.

Let's go through the mechanics of reading the cards here:

Top row: Read the cards in line for the situation. Second row: See the 4 cards as connectors between the pairs above them. Third row: See the 3 cards as pointing to the underlying structure of the situation. Fourth row: The bottom line. Create a synthesis that covers all the dimensions, from the descriptive (row 1), the analytical (row 2), and the reflective (row 3), to the evaluative (row 4). Finally, deliver a message as coherently and concisely as possible.

ROY DE DENIER
VALET DE DENIER
ST GERMAIN
ILE M AVELBOURY
IEAN NOBLE
ROYNE DE DENIER
LE IVGEMENT
XX
CHE VALIER DESPEE
X
VII
VII
XVIIII
LE SOLEIL
II
II
IIII
IIII

The X marks the spot. Note that since we're dealing with a general question, the cards determine 'who is doing what to whom,' according to the rule of thumb of looking at what is possible and plausible in the given context. Let's have the question again: 'what is at stake in finding my place in the world?' You're welcome to think of this question also in terms of figuring out what you're best at, so you don't waste time with trying to fit into an environment that demands something other than what you can offer at the most of your potential, education, and skills.

Based on the cards here we could say something like this: 'you must realize that what you possess (KCo) is subject (PCo) to negotiation and bonds (2Co) that you make according to what you like (5Cu) and the value you can create for others (8Co). Those who are like you (QCo) will find you (XX). Some will challenge your belonging (KnS), but since what you have to give comes from the heart (5Cu), your territory is covered (10Co). Finding your spot in the sun is informed by work and conflict. The bottom line is to recognize what sits in the 4 corners of your world, and formulate from there your own core principles.'

THE 'MEANINGLESS' DRIVEN READING

Earlier in this book I talked about the pips as markers for grammatical coherence. For example, I can say the following, just by looking at a string of three cards, 5 Swords, 10 Cups, 8 Batons: 'however much I dislike parties, there's a time when I need to reflect on their function.'

 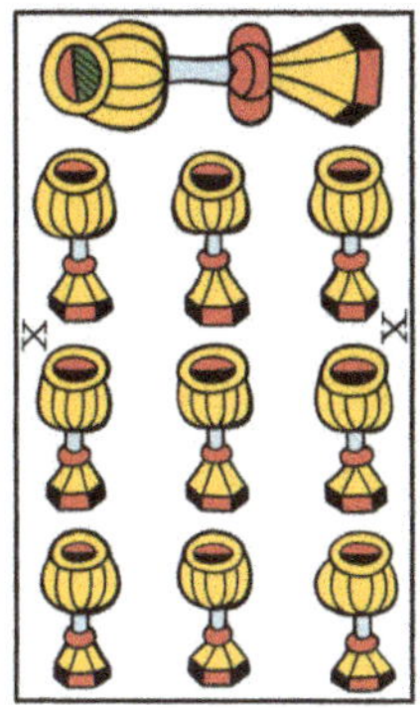 

This line can be given in response to a question about how to accept drama and the public circus that comes with it. Not everyone can see value in going to parties. As you can see, this reading is driven by the 'meaningless' approach, where I don't immediately think: 5 is for the body, as we have 5 limbs; with the swords it must be about dislikes; 10 is about a whole lot of drinking, and 8 batons about what the hell to do about it. My reading here is thus driven by context and nuanced by what I can logically infer about my action-oriented goals.

What we can also do is not only look at how we can punctuate our readings with the pip cards, but also at how we can calibrate them. The nuance in the previous example was clear: we went from 'what can I do about it' to reflecting specifically on the function of parties. The 8 Batons at the end of the string doesn't mean, 'it's going bad.' It simply means that you now have an opportunity to turn your painful resistance into something you can use.

The tens in a reading don't just put an end to it – the 10 of Cups always spelling it out for me: 'enough of this already' –

but they also give us insight into how we can move from the idea of merely dropping everything — 'it's done' — to dropping it in favor of changing the approach through recalibration. The 8 Batons in my example was not merely about 'plans,' but more about seeing the value of function in context.

So there's quite a difference between the reading that's driven by context and the meaningless card that, however, makes perfect sense, and the reading that's driven by general keywords and straight cliché and symbolic meanings.

Now let's perform some snappy readings for these three concepts, as they are perfect examples of not only what we can encounter on a daily basis as common concerns, but also of what we can see the court and the pip cards do when they raise the quality and nuance of our readings.

As most are pressed for time and the demand to deliver impeccable work, most end up procrastinating doing anything at all for fear of critique. The consequence is guilt and an inability to pardon yourself.

Let's take PERFECTIONISM first in an example of a useful question that you can ask your cards, or one that you can help others to formulate. I'll use my own nephew to illustrate in all the three instances. At the time of this reading he was a young man of 23 and very talented, a musician and a bit of a language genius. He dropped the dream of becoming a concert pianist because he couldn't be sure to be perfect. He enrolled in a language program at Copenhagen University, but he then couldn't see the point of studying Polish to perfection. 'Who needs to be that special?' Due to lack of high dedication to anything, because of high self-expectation, he developed anxiety. What to do about it? So he asked me: 'what goals can I set for myself that will bypass my desire to be perfect?' As usual, the cards delivered an apt sequence of images to consider.

I said the following: 'whether you can feel the love of the one who has your back or not is irrelevant. You don't live on impressions. Your goal is to take control of your mind, not let the mind take control of you. Enslaving yourself to the grand demon of perfectionism is not the way forward. Swing your baton over the Devil's head, and get on with the imperfect program. You're never perfect because no one else is.'

The implicit in this reading is also an answer to what was not put on the table as part of the question, but the cards gave us an idea as to what the starting point was. The man of love, King of Cups, backs the young man. But can he see that? He cannot. He advances towards the Devil that features many eyes, on his belly too. Why? Because there's lack of vision here.

Let's now turn to PROCRASTINATION. The question here is the following: 'I know I have to finish my BA project after having postponed it already, but innermost I prefer not to. How can I get past the situation described in Melville's short story: *Bartleby the Scrivener?*' I plead guilty here, as I scared the crap out of my nephew with prophesying that if he doesn't deal with 'I prefer not to', he'll end up like Bartleby... so his question was informed by this sad, horror story.

On this I said the following: 'the man of love is here again. Cut out your impressions of who watches you, whether this be your father or your mentor. Essentialize, and then essentialize some more. If you make your cuts in accordance, and *not* base them on emotional content, then you can discard what holds you back. The answer to the problem of procrastination is in recognizing just what this is, without judging it, and in how you then essentialize to what needs to be done. Beware though of going from moderate to increased pain unnecessarily.'

Let's now take the final example here, and look at PARDON-
ING. For this related, follow-up question regarding my nephew's predicament, we got this formulation: 'how can I pardon
myself, when I fail to show up for myself and others?'

The answer here was: 'you can't. Not as long as you turn
your back from the professionals who are willing to help you
and are competent in doing so. The Pope *can* absolve, and the
mother *can* understand and offer support. There's valuable advice in the world, both of the spiritual kind and also of the
pragmatic kind. Let go of your guard and belligerent attitude.
Seeking pardoning starts with honesty, with seeing what *is,* not
with the shame that you impose on yourself. You need to nail
your project? Do it. Don't think of it as nailing it perfectly.
Just nail it, without adding modifying qualifiers to the act.'

One year down the road, the nephew changed lanes again,
and embarked on a new course of study: optometrist, going
for a masters in neuroscience. The many eyes on the Devil…

As we've seen, agency was given here in the context of a young man's struggle. When more than one court card were in play, I've assigned the power to act according to the rule of distribution aligned with age and gender. Usually the King of Cups is an older blood relation, or someone we hold in highly intimate regard, such as a mentor. Pages are young subjects. When the knights are in play we talk about the subject actively engaged in participating in the unfolding of events.

The 'meaning' of the trumps is assigned according to the function of each trump in context. The Pope gives advice and comforting counsel, while the Empress rules and dictates. The Devil is the Devil, enslaving others, often making them believe that there's no alternative to whatever grievance, other than taking the path of manipulation and deceit. The number cards give us a sense of how stretched the elastic is. With the swords the tension is painful and cutting. Cups release the tension. Batons make it exciting. Coins transact for it: 'if you show me yours, I'll show you mine.'

There's more in the power of the pip and court cards, when we observe the interplay between agency, rulership and timing, when we see the cards as coherent markers of morphological and semantic significance. Our stretched elastic gives us a sense of how cultural positioning impacts on connectors and topical bridges. We can look at cards as available slots: when can you say it? How do you say it? Why do you say it? What conditions are the cards in? How do they mark a predisposition? If you want brilliant readings, you have to polish them into a diamond, according to your own justice.

Wishing Well

EVERYBODY IS FAMILIAR with the Buddhist greeting: 'may all sentient beings be happy.' The Christians also say, 'I'll pray for you', if they hear you're in trouble. 'May you live 10000 years,' the Japanese shout, martial arts style, when they want to cheer with a hurrah. Some African and Arabic cultures greet women with these words: 'may you have many children.' Now, if you thought of taking any of these wishes literally, I bet you'd be horrified.

The truth is that we can never generalize. What is happiness for some is disaster for others. Some get high adrenaline from being in trouble, while making it to 80 without any trouble is a tall order. Not to mention the number of emancipated women I know from African and Arabic cultures for whom the idea of having any children at all is already is enough to cause suicidal anxiety. What does it mean to pray for others, and how beneficial is it? We leave this question of ethics aside, as it's not the most interesting. What is interesting is this: how can we mean what we say, even if the saying is part of innocent — we think — cultural encounters and exchange? We want to know this, because it's relevant for divination. Not all who consult us mean what they say, and that can reflect in the cards.

'It's about emptying the house,' you hear old people say, while you also notice the mechanism of clinging to every possession like there was no tomorrow. Not to mention the fact that if you care to observe the actual behavior further, you will also notice that while the claim is made, five years down the road the place houses twice as many things as before.

People come to me with this concern: 'I want to stop procrastinating. How can I stop procrastinating selling the house?' As in the example before, with my nephew procrastinating, this is an actual problem for many others. So let's look at it again, from a different angle and cartomantic point of view. Before I lay down any cards, I ask the people interested in knowing how they can stop procrastinating: 'how much do you actually mean it? Do you even know what it takes to actually mean it?' 'Err, what do you mean? I just want to stop procrastinating,' people say, looking at me in a baffled way.

I offer this thought: there's a difference between wishing for it, being motivated for it, and having an intention for it. The trouble with wishing for something is that while it often discloses an intention, the wish is devoid of motivation. Just think: what motivates us to pray for people, to help them, to pray for ourselves, or to help ourselves? If we're not clear in the head as to what motivates us, there's one sure consequence: our intention to act on this motivation will be equally muddled. This leaves wishing altogether to the intangible realm.

When consulting the cards, the thing to remember is that some questions necessitate prerequisites, or awareness of a particular positioning. If you want to know how you can stop procrastinating, before you even ask that question, you must know something about what motivates you: what is implicit in your desire? Is the implicit motivation clear, so your intention will be clear? How connected is your motivation to your intention? Know this, *before* you read the cards.

Another procrastinator thus wanted to know: 'how can I mean what I say?' – as a prerequisite to reading the cards for the actual steps and strategy towards putting a stop to his idle situation.

Three cards fell on the table: 4 Batons, 8 Swords, 7 Batons. I said the following in a tirade: 'after constancy and painful expectation, there's release of action. It's normal to expect to mean what you say. But… You can only mean what you say, if you firmly check with your points of pressure, and then act upright and resolutely. How far does your elastic stretch? Before you stretch it, are your corners covered, and your feet well anchored in your motivation? You'd think it takes effort to maintain a solid stance. After all, saying that you mean something doesn't equal action, or immediate following through. But if action follows your words promptly, then you're set. You can mean what you say if you let the nerve of your intention stand in clear relation to your motivation. You can mean what you say when you let your word be unnerving and your action be unwavering. Don't think that you can beat yourself up about it, or stab yourself slowly and quietly in a cast iron cauldron. You can mean what you say in the exact moment you also show up for it. One way or another. There's no tomorrow. There's no promise: *I'll do it.* There's only stepping up to this reality: if you don't mean it, don't say it.'

Some might want to say, 'yes, that's a tirade, bordering on self-help counsel.' I don't have an answer to what others might say, as I'm not in the habit of projecting, and hence assuming anything. But I could say this: in a question of self-disciplining, what applies here is the old wisdom: 'no pain, no gain.' Bottling up resentment, to the point where just by looking at the 8 swollen swords in the middle here, is enough to make everybody think that we're about to witness an explosion.

Obviously it's better to step up to it ever so fast, that is to say, step up to the action that's called, 'I don't give a flying fuck about how conflicting my thought is.' So we're back to the same conclusion: you can mean what you say, if you intend to mean what you say, and then actually just say it like it is.

In what follows, we'll look at some applications of the basic principles of reading with the full deck of cards, and spot just the quirks that are interesting to spot in this vein here, where we wax poetic and philosophical against the background of psychologizing for the self, where focus on the self is relevant.

Humor Me

T HERE'S HARDLY ANY ASTROLOGY WEBSITE out there that doesn't emphasise the moods of the Moon. Let's see. I'm writing this while the Moon is in Libra, the sign of harmony, love, and money. The advice is to make sure not to alienate anyone by falling into some ambivalent trap, or what's worse, by making any contradictory claims. By the same token, if the Moon is in Leo, then the advice is to flatter people, give compliments, and engage in boosting everyone's ego. You do this, and they will like you. Very useful advice. But...

Someone please humor me: how does this type of advice, however useful, tie in with what I was just suggesting in the previous fragment about meaning what we say? If we pay compliments to people at a certain point in time because this time is ruled by planetary movements, then what does this say about our integrity at large, especially if we deem that now is a good idea to pay someone a compliment? What if the condition for such a gesture is right now, not a month from now? I'm not asking this question when the moon is in Libra today because I'm bent on going contrary to the useful advice – thus also running the risk of upsetting people – or because I want to express my sense of righteousness. I'm asking simply because I don't see how, if someone deserves a compliment for their looks when the Moon is in Virgo, then I can't do it because, according to the mood of the Moon, that would be the time to offer a critique instead, not a compliment.

What does it mean to adopt moods and humors that are not our own? Sometimes I have this discussion with my own astrology teacher, a very serious gentleman who only sends me emails when Mercury is not afflicted by some nasty aspect to the Moon or some other planet. This makes me think of the idea of constancy against the background of influencing others or manipulating them. Humors are the opposite of what we might think of as a constant and solid spine; one that doesn't bend in the direction of giving people what they want to hear all the time.

I'm not advocating for an inflexible spine, as I can take my cue from nature: a bamboo tree bending in the wind will be infinitely stronger than the oak that doesn't. So constancy doesn't mean being inflexible. It simply means having a position that's aligned with your own humor completely independently of which direction the wind blows. But if you don't know what position you adopt, or even what humor you're in also according to what's available to you, then what?

No matter how much self-disciplining you impose on yourself where your strategies of self-empowerment are concerned, the truth is that you're always subject to internal and external conditions that may run completely counter to what you want to achieve. How do you figure it out? Some look at what others do. Imitating especially the best is always a good strategy, and even better if you can perfect their craft. But it becomes a lot less fair when you start comparing yourself to others in relation to what you project is personal business for you. The moment you take things personally, you become judgmental. Who will want to follow you when you're humoured like that?

A constant feature on the internet these days is related to growing an audience. Entire courses and workshops are offered on how you can humor others, which is also where observing planetary alignments along with your algorithmic stats comes in. In my reading practice, it's not uncommon that I get this question for the cards: 'how can I grow my Instagram, Twitter, or Facebook audience? How can I make more people visit my website so they can see my offerings?' I won't go into the countless types of advice to this effect, as the internet is already flooded with all sorts — 'roar' or 'use the art of suggestion and understatement,' they say — but I will point to what you may want to consider as a matter of course. A better question to ask is the question that opens you up to realizing that whatever impression arises in the mind, it is part and parcel of what you yourself project and perceive is the case.

Where does this leave the humor of others, or that of the Moon in terms of our indulging it? It leaves it to the world of alternative facts. In a way, a community invested in occult beliefs, cartomancy, astrology, and other divinatory arts is already a community of alternative facts. What makes it magical is precisely the alternative. The alternative doesn't prioritize solutions based on this reasoning: 'if people like you, they'll follow you, and then they'll buy everything from you. Just use an amplified voice. Be yourself.' Err... That's not how it works.

The alternative prioritizes the game of potentiality, the fact that while we may consider the moods of the Moon for the sake of the game, what we're up against is our own God-given sense of emptiness, of the blank surface that we can magically paint on in any way our linguistic competence helps us. Without the words to say it, there's no magic. Without words to think it, there's no imagination.

With this in mind, how about we ask the cards this question: 'how can I be constant against the shifting moods and positions of others? How can I remain immune in the face of *now they like me, now they don't?'*

In asking this I must disclose that I'm motivated particularly by young people who want to know, for whom I also read the cards a lot, contrary to expectation. But as I know this is something others who are in the middle of shifting lanes and careers also want to know, I'll let it stand here as it is, disclosing all the present and, notwithstanding, absently articulated anxieties. Let's see what the cards say:

The Page of Coins, 3 Coins, King of Cups, and Queen of Coins make an appearance. For this one I said the following: 'some assets you show, some you don't. You can remain constant when you bank on symmetrical relationships. If you give one, the other must give one. What is buried in the ground, can stay in the ground. You can think of your third coin as insurance against the time when the one who used to like you, now turns his back at you in order to seek the favour of the one who is older and more interesting financially.

You can't control what people like or dislike. The best is to know that you yourself can be above likes and dislikes. Make your transactions in accordance. If 'liking' happens, it happens, and if it doesn't, it doesn't. It may well be that your audience won't grow if there's dislike of what you have to offer, but if you're above liking and disliking, how is that going to affect you? Connect with your inner glow. Let the underground valuable turn into a king's purse. If money happens, it happens, and if it doesn't, it doesn't. You are not the money you make, or the money you have. That is your constant. That is your undivided mind.'

In this reading what we note are also the pairs. There's a certain symmetry here that invites us to consider precisely the transactional idea already inherent in the question: 'what can I give in return for acceptance and goodwill?'

A coin plus one in the ground for three coins. Small change. A big cup for a big coin. Big exchange. By looking at these cards we can say that the ones with the best knowledge of what they have in their hand win. So the invariable advice here would be to say that if you cultivate your own gift, so that it has an unambiguous value, then chances are that you can win at the game of exchange. There's isn't a person out there who will not want what you have to offer, if what you have to offer is solid. Fluff can only reach so far…

Believable Stories

I F WE CAN ESTABLISH that what we do is not subject to likes and dislikes, then we can think about what we know, how sharp our knowledge is, what stories we create based on what we know, and how believable these stories are. I like the idea of sharpness here simply because, let's face it, armed with a sharp object you're very believable. Imagine having a confrontation. You have a shiny blade in your hand. The other holds a coin. Imagine saying to the one with the coin in her hand: 'how do you like this?' Or, 'how much do you dislike this?' The other would think you're probably stupid to ask about likes and dislikes. She may even blurt at you: 'what's it to you whether I like this or not? You're a warrior, not an aesthete. Come and get me.' This would be a normal reaction to your context. As a warrior you normally create a story of threat, strategy, and war. You can't be bought and you can't be seduced. Thus, what the other one sees is the potential that you chop her up and then run with her coin too. This is a very believable story, also because it happens all the time. Repetition creates icons and stereotypes.

Some stories are created beyond the possibility to negotiate. They have value by virtue of being believable. I'm fascinated by stories of samurai. Especially the part when they walk about, and then live and die even without ever having had to draw their sword. People watch them from afar, from what they consider is a safe distance. This watching has the character of a declarative statement: 'I believe you.'

The samurai and the figure of the ronin, or the unattached swordsman, have entered our collective memory and popular culture by telling what is essentially a very basic story anchored in projected and imaginary dialogues that have a simple exchange as their premise.

The samurai King: 'I can cut you'. The clever Queen: 'I believe you.' End of business. Each minds their own. Now, when it becomes interesting is when the other covets what the samurai knows. While a merchant, man or woman, is more prone to negotiation: 'my coin for your sword?' a warrior is not. 'Are you kidding me? Not a chance.'

The solution is to propose discipleship. Sometimes the samurai agrees: 'Ok, I'll teach you.' But when this happens you'll see that it always starts on a premise of establishing negative value, with the samurai being *not at all* interested in who or what you are, and what you think of him. I get a kick out of having figured it out for myself that what the samurai knows best is how to say NO. He says NO to a life of dictations by saying YES to death, the ultimate negation of life and all cultural conventions whether they be determined by rank, gender, age, or race.

As this is a territory I've been exploring for some time now in my work with cards and Zen, I won't go into the many fascinating details about it, but I want to offer here a snippet of insight into what I take from such cutting lessons, as it relates to how we create believable stories (if your interest is piqued, however, consult *What is Not: Marseille Tarot à la Carte*).

The point I'm after is related to how divination, as stated earlier, sits on the enchanted domain called 'magic with words.' First we name the problem, and then we let the cards name the solution. We may think that we look at visual imagery when we have the cards on the table, symbols invested in power games, but the reality is that what we're looking at is our own language, and how the glyphs we give voice to inform our mundane experiences. So when I go sounding like a culture critic, marketing critic, or a critic of the occult – critic in the academic sense of a person who analyzes phenomena and offers an evaluation – what I do is highlight what we can expect in the form of a question from the people we work with.

I can't stress this strongly enough, the fact that people come to the fortuneteller when the other consecrated professions don't work for them any longer. When the shrink or the cognitive psychologist takes too long to make a point, the cards offer a very useful short cut to both the problem and the solution. When the financial adviser fails in his prediction on how the stocks fair on the market, the cards offer surprising alternatives. When the boss flatters you, but does nothing to promote your actual skills, the cards can be very blunt in suggesting just what the slashing of the throat may look like – his, not yours. When people you work with start false rumors about you, because they can't stand your drive and capacity to mind your own business, the cards spell out how their hypocrisy could be denounced. People put on the fortuneteller's table what moves in them, when it's not the holy ghost, and then expect to see the only sincerity available, when everything else is contaminated by false morality, righteousness and entitlements, crass stupidity, and regular mental imbalance.

In my whole career as a fortuneteller, what I've been after is one reaction only from the sitters: 'yes, this,' they must say, pointing to what I myself point to. Enough of, 'first I kiss you and then I cut you'. That's not a good transaction, if you're the recipient of these words. What you want to hear from the cards is how you can turn your words around, and hence your world.

Let's look at some context first, given the above premise, and then read a 9-card tableau for the situation. Now, what I appreciate about the magical community is that it's filled with creative and innovative people. Many are successful entrepreneurs with whom I often have marketing conversations. Most are into YES, into creating so-called positive value. I say NO. This is my magical weapon for many wars. Not that I go to war all the time, but I like the idea of following whatever I have come to realize about my nature. I don't follow dictations.

Since I left academia for the less prestigious job of working for myself, I've been confronted with many fears. Not mine, to be sure, as I say NO to fear, but others. 'You must do this or that, say yes to this, yes to that, say yes to your customers, say yes to what *you* want, say yes to what *they* want,' and so the story goes. All fine up to the point when I'm strongly advised to address people directly, call them by their names (or let a newsletter algorithm do that for me), address their individual needs, imagine what they desire, and bow to the illusion that 'it's all about them'.

Well, you see, I don't fall for automated marketing emails that start with, 'Camelia, you've gotta hear this,' marketing that assumes to know what I want, what I struggle with, what my needs are, and what I imagine about embodying a particular desired identity, if any at all. Just as I don't get impressed by such tactics, I can't imagine anyone I address in my own email campaigns does. So I don't. I don't assume. In other words, I find myself following absolutely none of the strategies that marketing gurus out there devise in the name of surviving in business. I pretty much say NO to all of it. I say NO to the idea of catering to imaginary clients and potential clients. A potential client is exactly that, potential, not reality.

My own so-called surviving strategy has been very simple: 'those who are like me, will find me.' I don't put any effort into imagining who, out there, might be my potential client, who might read this book, who might take my cartomancy classes. I do what I do and fling it to the public to the best of my ability. If people want it, excellent. If they don't want it, excellent. There's no difference in my attitude towards what I expect. Because I expect exactly nothing. What I put energy into is *what* I create and *how well.* No one can be a better judge than myself of what I create, how masterfully, and where it all comes from. This premise alone means that I entertain no illusion about how many or who exactly I *reach,* simply because I'm always alone in what I do and what I think.

I don't fall for the illusion of *community,* as interestingly enough, when it comes down to it, we observe that the community minds its own business at a very individual level, in spite of contrary claims. Last I've checked, communities are not exactly Zen.

Valuing this aloneness means a great deal, as it affords you the space that's completely devoid of making assumptions and presumptions. Second-guessing is not an option either. This also means that, in principle, nothing of what you create and put out there into the world is ever up to negotiation. You think it is, but in reality it isn't. Imagine living with this realization, and consequently just doing your thing and entertaining zero concerns about potential responses, whether positive or negative. You can call this a conscious act of embodying the attitude of 'take it or leave it.' Why does this work? Simply because of the realization that if there's feedback or response to what you create, then this particular feedback or response will also very much be the manifestation of someone else's aloneness – even when this aloneness happens that it's the expression of some consensus opinion.

If a hundred people consume your offerings, you can have one hundred percent confidence that, at the end of the day, what you sit with is a hundred opinions, impressions, critique, or praise. So much for being purposeful in your business and reaching the one and only… The way in which we perceive the world is not through an assessment of the world such as it is, but rather through the realization that what we perceive at any given time is our own perception of perception.

In its undiluted form, Zen teaches that we don't perceive the world. We perceive our perception of the world. So we're always one level lower than 'the thing itself.' Given this realization, it makes very little sense to me to create anything in the name of what I perceive that even my own desire is. As far as I'm concerned, I try to not have any desire. I just do what I perceive I'm good at, which is to give sharp advice, say no, transact for no illusion, and expect no miracle. The only miracle that excites me is the nothingness of it all; the fact that nothing has any substance. Given this premise, I like to move mountains, speak to their silent wisdom, and pulverize the hell out of expectation. I practice entering the void because that is my vehicle to the absolute beyond. In this state of mind, there's no mind, there's no compromise, there's no 'be careful not to offend,' there's no illusion. Things are as they are. Take it or leave it.

Cards are like calligraphy. They can disclose the nature of the self when the self is beyond the fear of rising to expectations. This is bad for the mind that will always find strategies of trumping the nature of the self by creating anxiety. Pip cards and court cards are like the dots that connect the major narrative lines puncturing them with the unexpected. In the context of working for yourself, what questions do you ask your cards in your strategy of going about it, of creating stories that are not just believable, but also entirely true to you?

Are your questions *client* related? Who are my people? What do they want?

Are your questions *product* related? What am I selling? What is the value of what I'm selling?

Are your questions *problem* related? What problems do I imagine I'm solving? Is my effort informed by any 'savior' syndrome that I also imagine matches what I promise?

Are your questions *distribution* related? How is my image and that of my product in the world, on social media, or some other such channels? What narrative does my product tell? What story do I invest in?

Lastly, are your questions *self* related, or *other* related? What illusions do I maintain? How prone am I to falling for slogans such as: 'it's all about them', 'the customer is always right,' 'know everything about your customer,' 'be ruthless'? What is my vehicle to the realization of truth, which is another way of asking, what is my vehicle towards seeing things as they are?

Sometimes I run a check with myself and read a set of three cards for each of these questions, or some other similar ones. Though I have to admit that since my philosophy is simple and rather one-sided as I don't negotiate much, what I check is just strength. I check the strength of my attitude of 'take it or leave it,' as I don't want it to be the manifestation of indifference or even resentment. I check the strength of my acceptance of what is, whether this is feedback that translates into monetary value and appreciation, or critique. I check the strength of my fearlessness and what informs my discernment. If I'm prudent, what is this attitude a manifestation of? Fear, or wisdom?

Doing a 9-card reading for these considerations can be rewarding, as you get to see the dynamics of morphing: your attitude and perception morphing with the state of things such as they are, not such as they are part of whatever narrative you serve yourself. Here's an example of a question that combines interrelated statements, one about your skills, another about your attitude towards what you do with your skills, and a third about your concern with *how* what you do is received by the public. Disregard this latter concern, however, if your business has a Zen-oriented premise, insofar as any meditation practice that has self-analysis in focus maintains no illusion of separation between 'you' and 'them.' Thus, let us ask the cards the following: 'what is the best business strategy for me beyond mainstream marketing dictations?' and 'what is my vehicle towards embodying a completely fearless attitude towards what I'm creating, for what purpose and for whom?'

Before we proceed with the reading of the cards here, it may be helpful to keep in mind that although we talk about having a 'purpose' and 'direction,' what we're actually talking about when we use such concepts is just a mirror of what we project is the manifestation of our aims. In reality, 'purpose' and 'direction' are words that belong to the register that gives us more cause for anxiety than comfort. They are not invested in our ideal attitude towards maintaining neutrality vis-à-vis our identifications with the image of the self that we create, an image that is always arbitrary and dependent on shifting contexts for self-realization. Finally, let's look at our 9 cards on the table, as this tableau is actually quite fun to go through.

ROYNE·DESPEE·

LLBATELEVR

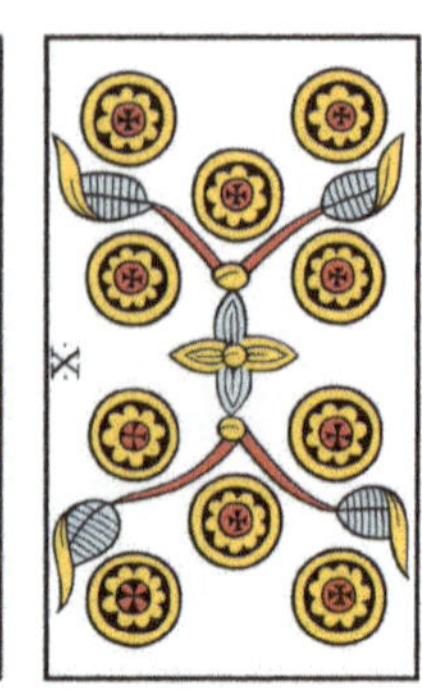

X·

III

CHEVALIERDESPEE

VIII

IVSTICE

ROYNE·DEDENIER

CHEVALIERDEDENIERS

ROYNE·DECOVPES

The Queen of Spades has turned her back from having an emotional conversation with the Magician. 'I've had it', the 10 Cups suggest – here's your first connector acting as a full stop. While the two can be said to have been in agreement at some point, they entertain no illusions now – though the Magician still makes a living selling it by virtue of his very function.

There's money to be made, and there's drive towards it. While the Knight of Swords charges ahead, ready to dig for the coin that's not in conversation with the two above it, Justice has no opinion about it. The Knight can trust her to back him, however, as we can infer that, with Justice in his line, he can now make the right decision. This may be useful, as you never know with the swords people and how much they ultimately dig financial interests; they are more prone to sabotaging them. Here I like the suggestion that if you know the value of what you're offering, and you're fair about it, then the only natural thing that you can expect to happen is to get more of it. Your business and cash can simply flow if you abide in truth and stand your ground unsentimentally.

The Queen of Coins has the necessary experience. We see this from her position, turned not towards the one making an offering, but rather turned towards the void. That is her confidence, namely, that she can afford to stare into the void. She holds up her own coin in a gesture that makes us think that she's ready to add to the three above her.

If you have experience, you don't need to worry about what happens when your working power is exchanged for pleasure. You will work because you love it. The last conversation here between the Knight of Batons and the Queen of Cups testifies to that.

I can't help but laugh a little at the middle column: the Magician knows how to move mountains, how to make the swordsman act in accordance with his will or magical power. Running a business *is* knowing the power of magic, knowing the power of the samurai, the power of fairness, the power of the coin and the sword forged in fire, and the power of love. The best business strategy is this: do what you love and abide in justice. Abiding in truth is not about emotional narratives, melodrama and vulnerable stories that sell. It's not about boosting 'big me,' impaling 'small me,' or flattering 'important you.' It's about flow, the flow of nothingness whence moving mountains is not even a big deal, but something that you do every time as a matter of course, effortlessly and completely fearlessly.

As for nuance, you can ask yourself this: a sword for three coins? A cup for a baton? What's the difference? Incidentally, it's not for nothing that Justice presides over the Queen of Cups, whom gravity pulls towards where trustworthiness is concerned. You *can* cut somebody into halves as an act of loving kindness…

Insofar as this tableau begins with the Queen of Swords, who is traditionally associated with the opposite of trust, and ends with the Queen of Cups, who is associated with benevolence, we can further argue that what makes your business strategy successful here is your ability to tell a believable story that inspires. But there's a catch. You may have a clear a vision of your goals, a cutting-edge focus, and strong determination, but if you don't know how persistence works *with* change, not against it, then you don't know the value of your own story.

By saying NO to con men, you say YES to the discerning factor. You can *know* what a Magician does, and use his shape-shifting ability to your own ends, but you can also *know* that you can do better, when you combine showmanship with absolute faith in the fact that, ultimately, life flows and it happens exactly as it happens, quite independently of what you make of it. The believable story is, after all, a mirror you hold up to others. Meanwhile, what you can do for yourself is exercise the art of kindness, in love and war alike.

Wait for It

W HEN WE SAY, 'I'M OUT OF TIME,' we don't always refer to being unable to complete a task according to schedule. 'I'm out of time' can also refer to a sense of escaping time. Being out of time in this sense means being beyond change. But being beyond change does not mean being beyond expectation. As you cannot experience being out of time in the sense of being out of it, as in, being beyond consciousness, or dead, you cannot escape having some sort of expectation. After all, experience generates more experience, not a reconciliation of opposites.

The interesting thing about waiting is that when you do it, you can, at the same time, witness how your experience of what you expect generates more experience of what you can both live and imagine at the same time. Just think: the more you wait for something that's anticipated by your senses, the more your adrenaline gets you out of yourself in the sense of placing you besides yourself. If prolonged, this act of waiting for your senses to realize themselves through mundane channels of manifestation turns into nostalgia of various degrees, ranging from romantic feeling and melancholia to obsessive pathology. Note that the senses are *not* your emotions about them. If you want to know what I'm talking about, beyond taking this as a point of academic discussion, then bring to your mind a time when you were in love. When you're in love you're out of time. We don't love with our emotions, as most people think. We love with the heart. Quite literally, when we're in love we experience waiting for the lover with a lot of blood pumping through our hearts. This is not an emotional response to love, but rather very much a somatic one.

The same applies to eating a dish that makes you swoon, or to listening to a piece of music that transposes you somewhere that's quite unbelievable. There's a whole science on waves carrying out sound vibrations to places that usually connect you to a piece of memory, smell, touch, or other sensorial impressions. It is for this reason that we can consider waiting for something with all our senses one of the most poetical acts; also because when things go wrong, it's not because of the senses, but because of the emotions that mess up the senses. It can be pretty disastrous to remember the taste of vinegar as something sweet. But just think: in the context of reading cards for love questions, how many times have you come across this very situation, when a woman, for instance, remembers her abusive relationship as something soothing and comforting, thereby being ready to continue in her imagination to entertain the idea and hope that her lost 'lover' will someday return to her.

There's a lot of anxiety in the world. Part of it has to do with how we register and archive our sensorial impressions, and the fact that we end up waiting for the wrong thing. The other part relates to the fact that most have lost the ability to wait altogether. Even popular sayings that used to be associated with virtue are now considered fatalistic: 'all good things happen to those who wait' is now a phrase that many scoff at, forgetting that the implication of this saying is far more interesting than the reason for its dismissal, one that has to do with prioritizing action over inaction.

Waiting is also an act, of course. To forget that means to forget what action really is, namely, the process of doing something. The process of doing something is not 'success', as many fallaciously believe, but rather, performing a deed. When you just wait, and don't think about it, thus distorting your waiting with memories of stories that can turn more and more colorful, what you do is place yourself beyond time. In this sense the saying, 'all good things happen to those who wait,' expresses waiting beyond change, which is time's corollary.

When your waiting bypasses your memory, you find that it acquires the quality of symbolic and non-verbal communication. Linguistic competence, eloquence, and analysis turn into a kind of poetry that is the manifestation of what's closest to your senses when they express themselves. In other words, you find that when your waiting is poetic, and therefore symbolic, as it's not tied with your verbal language of desire, you can easily wait even for that which you lack the words to say or for that which you think you need time to unfold.

Now some would ask: if you can't be explicit about what you want, how can you develop any strategies of waiting for it? This is a good question, and the answer is that you can't. But when we talk about forms of mysticism and personal gnosis, then we're with the possibility of knowing things beyond the words. Such knowing is usually the result of first struggling with ambiguity (poetic language is always ambiguous), and then with exorcising scepticism out if its limits (logical language is always about that). While waiting beyond the words that can articulate what you're waiting for is always a transgressive act, it has a very pragmatic function, namely, that of knocking off all your illusions about your emotions and how exactly they relate to the realm of the senses.

Speaking on the mundane level, you can, for instance, have the sense that you're done with the work you're doing now. You can even observe how your body rejects that work, with your kidneys and bladder not being able to regulate the pee anymore. You ignore this subtle message because you're emotional about changing lanes. After all, you've invested more than 25 years in your career. You go to the doctor's for a remedy, while entertaining the illusion that if only you can keep going, you'll enjoy success.

But what if there's another alternative? If you're tired of being on time, of being on beat, and of the call 'action, action, action' that completely disregards all your senses, then you may want to ask your cards this question: 'how can I get better at waiting? How can I place myself out of conventional time, so that when I eat, I eat, when I sleep, I sleep, when I make love, I make love, without at the same time investing myself in other, side narratives than the simple ones I'm already engaged in sensually creating?'

Before you lay down any cards to investigate, think of the following: if you get pip cards and court cards, think of them as connectors to your ability to wait with all your senses whether this waiting is for something clearly defined, or for something that transgresses the normative codes. Don't think in cliché divisions, à la 'cups are for love,' or 'coins are business.' If you ever read erotica literature, or watched a French film from the 60s on the play of gazes, then you'll know how much love a piercing sword can possess, or how sublime a conductor's baton can make music sound in your ears. A quick look at the question posed here based on a reading of three cards can disclose the following:

5 Cups, King of Cups, and 8 Batons speak theirs: no matter how self-indulgent it may appear, the best way to wait for something to unfold naturally is through distancing yourself from making any rigid identifications with the thing you're waiting for. Two cards here emphasize two different stages of flow: one is dynamic, 4 cups get together to celebrate the 1 in the middle. The other is static, we take note of the decorated cup in the hands of a King. Clearly there's a rhyming scheme here to remark, as we connect the cup in the middle of the 5 Cups card with the one in the King of Cups card.

The flow that has two natures can create a story. The King says the following to a gathering of grossly intertwined sticks: 'this cup here, look at it, it's special. You can't have it. Not only that but I'm the one who helped it turn into a thing of beauty, thus separating itself from the others.' What I find enticing here is the gesture of the King: free hand on hip, and legs turned towards the cards that depict the more immediate senses, the ones that have flow embedded into their nature. He acknowledges the pressure from the batons: 'you got a special cup, what are you going to do with it, what is its purpose?'

This King is clueless. The King of Cups is not into those kind of disciplining calculations. He is an aesthete. Dionysus of the senses, not of structural planning. If anything, he *is* the very representative of the suit of pleasure. The message that we can take from this is clear: you can get good at waiting, at focusing on just the one 'special' thing that you hold in your hand, by completely disregarding the blocks building up in front of you. From the perspective of flow, where is there any space for the consideration of obstacles? What obstacles? Such questions are indeed most transgressive.

More generally, if you want to wax more than poetic, you can consider this philosophy: a cartomantic reading session with the full deck goes through four stages of recognizing what's happening: intensity, arousal of curiosity (though this can also have sexual content), nonsense and silence, and repetition. On this list I particularly like the last two: when the reader establishes intensity through reference to basic curiosity, 'nonsense' takes over and articulates itself forcefully, yet paradoxically, through silence. There's always a moment in the reading session when both the reader and the sitter can be baffled, so they 'say' nothing. Because silence is instituted, there is thus a need for the repetition of all the other move-ments. This repetition is what constitutes transgression. While this transgression often comes close to being interpreted as a form of obsession – the reader is obsessed with decoding and the sitter is obsessed with the urgency to know things – it also ensures that something interesting happens between the reader, spinning off a story that the sitter brings to the table, and the sitter, whose story is often one of secrets.

The brilliant insight is that because transgression is what it is, a site of struggle and tension with language and ideas, it cannot *per se* also be the vehicle for communication as a result of precise readings (across and between the agents involved). In other words, everybody misreads everybody else – but not entirely. That's the beauty of cartomancy.

A reader may estimate a sitter's response quite accurately, but not because she is able to read her opponent with infallible precision – via classical cold reading or through the plain clar-ity of the cards – but because there is always a chance that she is wrong precisely and inasmuch as she is also right. I like this idea, especially as it relates to an ethical question: how much responsibility does the reader of cards have to show to their sitters? Here the correct answer must be this one: none.

Not a single nerve of responsibility must be shown, if wait-ing for the good thing to happen is to stand a chance of sur-vival in its intense, ravishing, illuminating, and for the most part violent mode – violent in the sense that such a waiting act violates the most basic cultural expectations, which is to wait for dictations from above to know what is appropriate and what is not, instead of just knowing due to seeing things as they are, and as they unfold in the ever-mysterious NOW.

Tarot cards are sensorial triggers. The trumps make us aware of the order of things, and they give us a blueprint for how we can transgress such orders. The pip cards and the courts connect us to the modalities of transgressing our inherent limits of being in the world.

You see the Ace of Spades? Now ask yourself without thinking of standard meanings: how many times was your sense of this card similar to this decision: 'That's it. Up until here, and no more?' Granted, some might also say: 'wait, isn't that the job of the 10 Swords, to make us realize that we've had it?' I would suggest that by the time we got to the 10 after the initial, ultimate decision was made, what we would actually say is this: 'I did it. I have fully realized the big NO. I'm now connected to the full stops of my life.'

'Is it better to wait with trying to find a better job?' someone once asked me, and got these two cards here. I said, 'yes, absolutely, wait exactly until you can't wait anymore.'

The Decisive Factor

MOST PEOPLE WHO HAVE BEEN FOLLOWING my cartomancy writings over the years have learnt that my least favorite card in the tarot pack is the Lovers. I keep coming back to this card, and almost always have bashing things to say about what it does in relation to the card it happens to be in play with. The big baton below says: 'it's here. Take it.' But does our Lover hear that? He never hears a thing; he never sees a thing; he never does a thing. You'd think a big offer like this would energize our anemic. It doesn't.

The standard meaning of this card is associated with love or choice. This is what I don't like about it already: regardless of what we say or mean about it, the card itself seems not to be able to make up its mind as to what it wants to represent beyond configuring forms of ambivalence.

Most people get excited, however, when the Lovers are in the picture. I get it, as this excitement ties in with the reason why we bother to reads cards at all: we read cards because we want guidance for our choices. Cards can show us alternatives; they indicate how we measure up in the game of comparing to others, they point to which way to go, they give us strong impressions of what we really like and what we really don't like. In other words, almost every reading session with the cards is all about what the decisive factor is when we need to make a choice. It's no wonder we get excited.

The Lovers shows up in your reading. Excellent. Now what? This card has the least potential to solve your problems. If auspicious at all, it tells you that you've reached a level of confrontation — some are in denial about that. How well do you know yourself? If you have to make a choice, is it based on knowing your mind, or is it based on hearsay, listening to the opinions of others? The answer to this lies in looking at what other cards, trumps and pips alike, you find nearby. As the Lovers will never give you clarity on what the decisive factor is when you find yourself at a crossroads, you need to figure out what you know about the value of things.

A decisive factor simply means possessing knowledge of a specific property. Lacking this knowledge leads to indecision, to more ambivalence. When you get this card, you get a signal that you need a resolve. Let's look at an example. You have a marriage proposal, or one that invites you to share your life with another. You know it in your heart that if you follow through, it will be a good thing. But you're not sure about what goes into making it stick. After all, so many divorce already three months after vowing eternal love.

If you were to know what they all thought on their wedding day, you'd find that many would say this: 'I did it because I knew it in my heart that this was the one.' But as things change all the time, and as history has also diligently been recording, the heart tends to possess a different kind of knowledge, taking place quite often immediately after the wedding night.

So what makes it stick? If you posed this question from the outset, you'd find that what you need is not to ask your heart about it, but rather, to know what your decisive factor is. Many would swear that what makes a relationship last is the intertwining of three essential properties: both parties have solid mental stability, both parties can provide solutions to problems that arise, and both parties can laugh together.

If you wanted your decision to be influenced by something more tangible than what the heart has to say, especially when it's in cliché mode, then you'd take your knowledge of such specific properties into account. Mental stability, ingenuity, and humor are often a safe bet. Others prefer passion, endurance, and honor. Have you ever thought of why the Lovers card features three figures on it, other than to tell us explicitly that here we're with an indecisive situation, with the young man in the middle hesitatingly asking himself: 'this woman to the left, or that one to the right?' Formally speaking we're here with a triangle, three variables that can lead to the determination of three winning factors that you can bet on – keep in mind though that, as there's never any guarantee for anything in life, what you do when you make a decision is never anything other than forecasting.

Ideally any choice is based on seeing both the explicit and implicit underlying structure of a matter. The explicit gives you focus. The implicit gives you perspective. Focus creates a sense of distinction; wide perception enhances play. This is enough already to keep you excited. But how do you avoid mixing up the levels? How do you know what your heart knows, either explicitly or implicitly, and which one is when?

I actually experience this very situation in my practice of reading cards that's a problem: people often present implicitly a predicament whose premise ought to be recognized as explicit, and vice versa. Many a time I want to ask them: can you please make up your mind about it? What do you really want to know? In strategies of decision-making this is bad. What can we do, then, to sharpen our vision as to what our decisive factor is, when the premise for what we want to know is not always clear?

A useful practice is to read a string of cards for the situation, and then select from your string the one card that you think is a 'problem' card, the one that necessitates knowledge of your decisive factor. This is standard practice if you mainly use the trumps in your readings, and only make recourse to the pip cards if you need clarification. Some call this following through 'the French school.'

The Lovers card is a usual suspect that often calls for the pip cards to 'clarify' it, but any other trump, pip card or court card can also pose a similar, challenging situation, and hence call for more pips on the table. With this 'problem' card in mind, what you can do is reshuffle your deck and do another reading with view to learning something about your trifecta, your winning order of the specific properties that speak in favour of your making a clear choice. Let me give an example based on a recent experience that has choice in focus.

As a lover of the samurai culture, aesthetics, and philosophy, there's no end to my love of the samurai sword. So I do the rounds in the antique collectors' world and educate myself as to which blade is the best that I can invest in according to what I can afford at a certain moment in time. One such blade was suddenly within my reach, and then out of my reach again due to inattention. I was vacationing with my family over the holidays and I got distracted. While thinking about returning to the sword in the middle of the family circus, as an excuse for not to, my superego also started censoring my desire with this question: 'what is the purpose of this collecting, anyway?' I gave in, even though I already knew that there isn't any purpose to anything whatsoever, and that in effect there's nothing I ever need. Not even food. I missed the boat on the 'purposeless' thing. The collector took the sword off the market quite suddenly.

The best part, however, is that this event gave me an opportunity to entertain myself. First, I observed my behavior around my reaction, ranging in emotion from 'oh no, this is what I get for my ambivalence,' to 'let's engage in a game of prediction and see what happened.' While the first manifested as regret, the latter manifested as joy in reading the cards about it. I even shared the story in the social media on Instagram — where's the fun in predicting if you have no witnesses? I formulated this question in three parts: did the Danish collector take his samurai sword off the market because: 1) I hesitated to put down $10.000 for it? 2) He sold it to another? 3) He regretted the decision to sell his precious possession?

Three cards fell on the table: the Knight of Batons, 2 Batons, and Temperance, and they had this to say:

'The collector was negotiating an offer, but the sword didn't change its status quo. He still has it.' Phew, I felt much better. I love the social media. People expressed their sympathy on this, along with their good wishes for another occasion. As I wanted some validation for my story and implicit prediction, I kept watching the collector's space. Meanwhile, I also had an occasion to practice the high art of Zen patience. My waiting time was rewarded. Two weeks later, the sword was back on the market.

The cards were correct on two out of the three points that I could verify: the *katana* was still with the collector, and the price was unchanged. If we assume that an offer was made, as the cards suggested judging by the presence of the eager Knight of Batons, now we can see that collector didn't take it. My blood pumped through my heart very fast: 'oh, such a fine Hizen blade from 1650… I'm not going to let it go again.' With the conditions changed towards favouring a second chance, I can say the following: while the heart was resolved in what it wanted beyond ambivalence, what was still missing was the decisive factor. What are the three specific properties that can speak in favour of making this investment?

One is scarcity and rarity. The second is the reasonable price that reflects the value of the sword. The third is indulging my youthful folly and not underestimating the power of useless things forming a collection. But what do the cards say? What is my decisive factor in buying the samurai sword according to the cards? Let's have a look at this personal reading, as it poses a few interesting aspects.

First, let us bear in mind that this question is also a setup, as it challenges me to recognize the possibility that whatever I also recognize as specific properties that can influence me in my decision can also align with saying no, rather than saying yes to it. A decisive factor can pull you in both directions, one where you go with it, and another where you go against it.

Second, note also that when I ask the question about what my decisive factor is in this given situation, I'm not merely asking a question led by modality, such as, 'why should I do this', as the answer can easily be one-sided: 'because I want to.' Possessing knowledge about the specific property of something is not the same as giving in to whims. In my desire and concern here, I want to know more about my motivation.

If I picked up where I left off, namely from my sense of relief at seeing Temperance signifying that the sword is still in the possession of the collector, we can now investigate into what this may suggest. In and of itself Temperance is associated with the virtue of moderation and regulation of flow. You're neither too excited, nor too indifferent.

With this in mind, let's pose the question again: what is my decisive factor?

Here come the Queen of Cups, 4 Coins, and the King of Batons. I laughed on two counts: first, while shuffling, the Queen of Cups fell out of the deck 4 times, before I laid down the cards. Yes, you heard that right, 4 times. Second, I laughed because every time the queen landed on the floor, I'd pick her up and put her back in the deck with this very thought in mind: 'because you want to.' I guess I insisted on putting the card back in the deck because I didn't want the situation of 'because you want to' to happen for no other reason than 'because I want to.' It goes to show: my poor ego had very little chance of winning over the power of my unconscious desire – or, well, conscious unconscious, as there was nothing innocent here that I wasn't already aware of. When this is said, let's see.

The decisive factor here *is* 'because I want to'. I may as well admit this as one of the specific properties that makes this sword worth the while. What I get to pay is not a lot. The 4 Coins card testifies to making a stable investment in line with what I can reasonably afford. The value of such swords is also a classic. People create value through the stories that they believe in. This has hardly ever anything to do with the thing itself. I'm not even sure one can put a price on a fine piece of steel made by a first or second-generation family of swordsmiths from the 1600s.

Let's continue with the cards: the man who sells the sword, the King of Batons, is not as sharp as the King of Swords. Perhaps he doesn't quite know what he's got there, though inveterate collectors tend to possess specific information. Where collectors are a bit 'special' is in their being consistently higher when it comes to valuing their collections. The interesting thing here is that neither the Queen, nor the King look at the money involved. Which is not a lot, again, all things considered. Why is that? What are they looking at instead?

Two more cards fell on the table, the Lovers and the Moon, each on the side of the Queen and the King, respectively.

The Queen is looking at the Lovers. Why am I not surprised? Here's our usual suspect, the initial ambivalence that started this whole story. In this light the Queen says, 'I'm not quite sure about this, but I still like it, monetary value or not.' The King is looking at the Moon. Is he mad to sell his sword at this relatively low price, or is he merely confused about it? I leave it to you to determine what you think my decisive factor pulled me towards.

❧

The overall point here is that what we can take from readings with the full deck is the following: whereas the trump cards describe a situation ever so explicitly, the subtler pip cards, featuring an arrangement of geometrical patterns that are not immediately intelligible to the eye, give us insight into the decisive factors that can go into influencing the situation at hand.

The court cards are the go-betweens, mediating between choice and decision-making, situations and their conditioning, polarities and the stretch of tension between extremes, and so on. We're still with the basic cut here, with the pip cards exhibiting their power by virtue of their connecting us to the way in which we understand the metaphors we live by. The ultimate question that the pip cards invite us to consider is always this one: how far do we stretch it, and for how long before the elastic bursts?

How sharp is *your* decisive factor?

Burning Bridges

ON'T BURN ALL YOUR BRIDGES, they say, without always thinking that before we burn any bridges there has to be a crossing of them first. How many do that? How many actually cross bridges before they burn them? How many cross bridges and then commit to this resolve: 'not only have I crossed the bridge, but I'm also going to burn it.' Bridges connect one thing to another. They are liminal spaces. Sometimes, however, these liminal spaces must be pulverized in order for something new to emerge.

Burning bridges is not always about regret. Quite the contrary. Sometimes they spell this out: there's only one path, to move forward, to keep going. You can make recourse to past memories, as it's not easy to vanquish them, whether they are good or bad, but you can also think of them in a detached way, in a way that's completely devoid of personal involvement. Why? Because whichever way you turn it, by default the only path is the way forward. The past does nothing for you. You can entertain yourself with analyzing 'what happened' and then with 'what happened afterwards,' but you can also remember that identifying with what happened, or clinging to what happened as a way of honouring your memory, leads to exactly nowhere. There's no virtue in honouring victimhood.

The good news about all connectors is that what is being brought forward in the combination of what is ahead of you with what is behind you has precisely the quality of forward-ness. There's only one path: moving forward. Defying flow, resisting, or turning back is a disgrace to your breath, to your potential to build bridges of your own. So far we've explored how the pip cards act as connectors, before they happen to mean anything. Take this example of a reversed victim story based on these cards: a power line-up consisting of the Queen of Batons, Ace of Batons, Force, and the Queen of Spades.

Little Red Riding Hood has an important task of delivery. Suddenly on her path she meets the big bad wolf. She takes out her blade hidden in her wooden scabbard that looks like a baton, and deals with it. End of story.

You can imagine who won. I think I see some hairs on the ground... Meanwhile, the Ace of Batons here doesn't mean 'new projects.' It simply acts as an adverb: 'suddenly...' Think: Batons are fast. The first is surprising. Ten of them are just tiresome already. The Queen of Batons's baton rhymes with the Queen of Swords's sword. Vitality turns into resoluteness: 'either I win, or the wolf wins. I prefer it that I win.' End of story.

Storytelling with cards is *not* a new invention, though sometimes you can come across ideas that present it as a new invention. Same thing with the obvious realization that what we do with the cards is create narratives that follow a particular sentence structure. 'Oh, so the cards can be about something other than inner psychology and personal gnosis?' 'Yes,' some answer in earnest to the question devoid of pretence, while others will hurry to take advantage of the situation and present sentence-making as the new holy cow in town.

There are bridges and bridges. Some are built across new and old wisdom, some are built across selfish interests. If you happen to realize that you've crossed the latter, burn it. Then keep going. If you philosophze with the cards, and others mistake this act with psychologizing, then point to their error first, and only then slash their throats, as you cross yet another bridge to burn.

Look at how things are connected in your practice of reading the cards. It's not about learning a 'new' method. It's about connecting the cards to a place that has to do with your ability to know context, to know what story you're in, and to know what place you have in the story. You are never 'just a reader of cards.' Sometimes you're Little Red Riding Hood, cutting right through it with her new samurai sword.

Free Will

MUCH OF MY TEACHING revolves around insisting on the significance of making preliminary assessments before any reading of the cards takes place. This includes looking at *how* people formulate what they put on your table. One of the most essential things that I do is always take that into account, as it gives me insight into what precisely it is that people cling to. If you practice enough, you'll see common themes and patterns emerging. The topical essays here very much revolve around what currently moves in society, what 'empowerments' our symbolic cultural structures invent, and what is promised. When none of that works anymore, the fortuneteller steps in. Most people who consult a fortuneteller cling to the illusion of 'control,' making recourse to that other big illusion called 'free will'. Compensating for what most perceive *is* a lack of control, you'll get to hear a lot of stories of guilt and victimhood.

Determining the degree of intensity of such stories can be a good idea. If the cards are already on the table, you can check with the elastic again: how stretched is it? The batons are a good indicator of this. How snappy? You're with the swords here. How lax? Welcome to the cups. How shiny and embellished? Here is the story of the coins. Sometimes I deliver this kind of message: 'there's nothing you can do about it'. I'm looking at these cards: 8 Swords, 4 Batons, the Hanged Man.

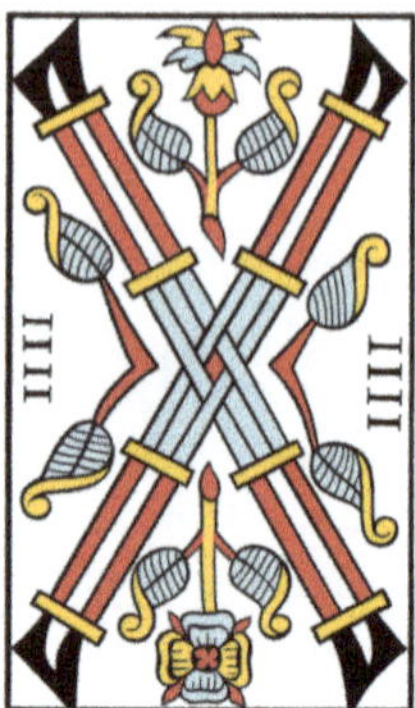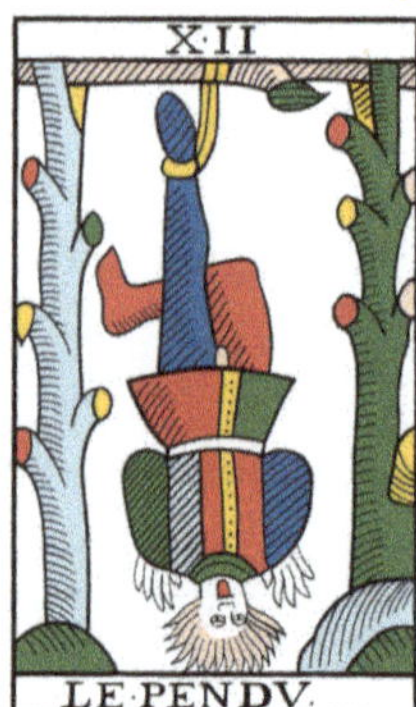

The other I read for is appalled. 'What do you mean? Surely your cards must point to the ways in which I can grow and transform...' The voice gets more and more desperate, which just happens to confirm my suspicion of the fact that, here I am, again, with a story about a desired identity, self-empowerment, and control, before an acknowledgment of what the situation is already exists. How can you transform anything as long as you're in denial about *what is already?* 'There's nothing you can do about it,' I insist. On occasion the other also insists, while slamming the door in my face, and walking out triumphantly: 'I have free will.'

I stick to my guns. I read the cards I get. If the other wants to talk about free will disguised as a desire to control, I cut her short and don't budge at all to accommodate her fantasy of transformation. We always do the things we do, quite independently of what we think is the personal, original, and creative clichés we like to serve ourselves. There's no such thing as an *authentic free-will self.* Life happens as it does, and the reality is that only what's under your nose counts. You can check the veracity of this if you ask yourself this question: 'am I reading these words because I decided to get this book, or am I reading these words simply because I happen to read them right here and right now?' What's under your nose is not for you to change, but for you to humbly observe and get on with the program in accordance. There's a lot of liberating power in this stance, as it relieves you of the thought that you have to *do* things, do things *differently,* rise to expectations unexpectedly, thus wasting a lot of precious breath.

In my reading sessions, I thus look at what people cling to, and start my readings from there. There's also a lot of discarding too: not this, not that, and not this other thing either. I go for the bare bones. In terms of action, if I give advice towards transformation, I look at this question too, as part of the preliminary process: what condition is this person I'm reading the cards for subject to? I don't fall for urgency: 'hells bells, tomorrow is Tuesday, Mars day, and you're so going to change this shit. You have free will.'

What is the certainty I'd speak with if I said that? Where would it come from? From seeing the future? From granting that we all have free will? From pointing to transformative mojo we can be lucky to have been born with? While I'll advise the person to act upon her free will on Tuesday, will she be able to see how life passes under her nose right now, without her making any effort? If I can't point to that, and make the other understand the exact implications of that, then I will do nothing other than participate in continuing her fears.

If I were to boil this down to one essence, I'd say the following: the reason why there *cannot* be any free will is because *now* trumps it; *now* in the sense of momentum, as in, right this moment. In our illusions to decide, change, even change perspective, transform, and whatever else we have in this register, what we actually do is live according to circumstance and condition. We don't change anything, but circumstance and condition can change for us. Free will presupposes consideration of the past, as in 'I won't do this anymore, as it's been bad for me,' with view to getting a better future, 'tomorrow I'll change tracks, and will feel much better.'

This is where I put people on the spot, people I read the cards for. I simply ask them, 'are the past and the future real?' when they insist that the cards give them something to compensate for, what the cards on the table already show they are in denial about. When the cards suggest to people: 'get real', they are not even kidding, the cards, that is. Neither the past, nor the future is real, so here's the million-dollar question in relation to temporality that we can all pose to ourselves: 'what would we exercise our free will against, when we eliminate the past and the future from the equation, an elimination that's necessary simply because both the past and the future are fictions, memories, or wishful thinking?'

There cannot be any free will because *now* always trumps it, leaving us no other option than to live life as life happens. The sooner we realize this, the more we get to live a life free of worry, arrogance, and personal impetus. It is in this observance of how life happens as it happens that we can locate the universal power of the pip cards, as it connects us to the biggest trump ever, the *now* that encompasses the functions and duties that we happen to fulfil in life: now I rule, now I race for success, now I retreat, now I slash throats, now I give, now I judge, now I hang, now I dream, now I love, now I am. The pips tell us how all these functions and duties are performed, and with what degree of energy or apathy, of stretching it or not, how fast or slow. Some dice are best rolled with a cold head. Some books are best read with a hot heart.

Let's look a meta-wish. Here's an example of a meta-wish: 'my wish is that all my wishes come true.' In some stories there's prohibition against meta-wishes, as they have a tendency to crash the system. But let's pretend we don't know that. Now let's ask the cards: 'I wish I had free will, how can I get it?' The implicit meta-wish here is this: if you have free will, then you can assume that everything you want, you'll get.

In a game with witnesses, I drew entirely at random these cards: 2 Cups, Queen of Coins, 8 Coins. They say the following: there's dualism in the world, one that makes us feel good, like a good wine in our cups transposing us to a place of comparison: 'my cup is half full, yours is half empty.' You must exchange this feel-good duality with one idea. What passes through your empty mirror? Many things align with what you see, like soldiers in some golden armor, and you can participate in this command: 'if you can think it, it exists.'

You *can* think 'free will,' and so it will exist. But is it real?

Further reading

For a wonderful discussion of meta-wishes and systems of beliefs crashing on our heads, see Douglas Hofstadter's celebrated book, *Gödel, Escher, Bach: An Eternal Golden Braid* (1999).

The Image Behind the Story

AS A TEACHER OF VISUAL TEXT (both in the academic context of art history and in the context of divination and fortunetelling), there are two principles that I hammer on: composition and connection. When we're presented with an image, it's often not enough to identify what's happening. For the experience that makes an impact, what we need is to connect what's happening to an emotional or rational response, or both, depending on our immediate context for viewing.

Whenever we connect the image to the emotion that we associate with the image, or the image to the decoding nerve, if we're with the detective kind of an investigation, what we're doing is create a story behind the image. It's for this reason that I always insist on considering the cards on the table as a possibility to connect the visual narrative frames with a story behind the frames. If Death is symbolically associated with 'the end,' when followed by another visual frame, say, the 2 Cups symbolically associated with courtship, we can say that, in the context of a relationship, we're talking about the dissolution of the friendship. This would constitute a reading of the surface level of the visual input from the cards.

In the context of connecting, however, we never simply go: 'the 2 Cups means the promise of marriage,' and 'Death means the end', as there's always a story behind the set of images we look at. If you only operate with the surface level of things, what appears to be the case is not always what you think.

In most European traditional schools of cartomancy, reading single cards has never made much sense, simply because judgments à la Death means Death are not very interesting. Within the Anglo-American tradition, getting Death as your 'daily' can settle a score. At least you can transform. But what's more interesting is how Death contributes to the unfolding of events, as in, 'what happened afterwards, when Death chopped the beloved heads?' or even, 'what was it like, this courtship, partnership, or *almost* marriage, before Death occurred?'

While card combination is the backbone method in traditional fortunetelling, from playing cards to the Tarot and on to other oracle cards, I wonder to what extent what is taken at surface level, for instance the idea that the combination 2 Cups + Death means the end of the marriage, can also be thought of as the principle behind crafting a story behind the level of the image-combination. Saying that a card, a combination of two cards, or a set spread 'means' something presupposes that there's a recognition of what is commonly agreed upon. But is what is commonly agreed upon also a dynamic process of crafting a story behind the image? Hardly.

Those familiar with my work and extensive writing on all the traditional cards for divination will know already about my disdain for set phrasing in any form it may be presented. I often say that cards enable us to simplify things, and for many, divination now equals simplification *par excellence.* Here I can mention that the debate about this can get quite hot in the cartomantic community, with people discussing which among the cards are the most representative of the 'literal', and hence the presupposed simpler idea, as opposed to the complicated esoteric systems: Tarot, Lenormand, or Playing Cards?

I've had my say in this debate, the gist of it being that if something is simple or complicated, it's not found at the level of the image, but rather at the level of the approach one takes to the image. For instance, I like to think of my approach to reading cards as being informed, first, by observing the rules of formal design and composition as it connects to rhetoric and storytelling, and second, as being informed by martial arts in the Zen tradition of deconstructing language. Whether the tool I'm working with is called 'Tarot' or 'Lenormand' is completely irrelevant to me, because what I'm looking at is never 'meaning', à la 'this means that', but images that carry a story of functions situated in context.

When it comes to the simple, however, I think of what Einstein used to say, namely that a scientist should make things as simple as possible, but not any simpler. I think of the implications of *not any simpler* for divination. Simplifying a situation to the surface level is one thing. Crafting a story behind the image is another thing, as it forces us to think of cards and card combinations in dynamic ways that bypass any list of meanings whatsoever.

My own methodical approach has been to prioritize the function of a cultural precept over its symbolic counterpart, having an eye for *not any simpler*. In a given context, if 2 Cups + Death connects to emotion, then we can say that the story behind this combination is actually one of relief, as normally, people get a divorce because they want to, not because they have a fantasy about the value of the pain of having their relationship severed. Statistically speaking, the relief situation is much more predominant than the one in which the end of the marriage is a thing of sadness – these days divorce equals empowerment. This is fair, when it's about a welcome release, but sadly this type of an empowerment can also be the expression of the vulnerable as a commodity that is very much in vogue. You get married, cool. You get divorced, even cooler. Now you can show that you're human in your pain and misfortune.

Yet, in having internalized at surface level here that the 2 Cups + Death means the end of the marriage, the funny thing that happens is that, more often than not, the 'meaning' of this card combination is projected as a lamentable situation, even when it can be as plain as daylight that, indeed, there's no such thing as 'lamentable'. What interests me in my observation of this practice is how such a projection can be deemed efficient, in the process assuming also that helping with coping is what's needed. What would happen if we noted that, if just cause was on the table, what the diviner would need instead is pop the champagne for the sitter, and celebrate?

From my own practice, I can testify that whenever I had to pass judgment on the 2 Cups + Death situation in a question of a relationship, there was a lot more to gain by pointing to the relief factor, rather than sympathize with what I would assume is a pain in the neck of the other.

On this note, let me end here with a line of basic questions that you can think of, next time you have the full deck of cards in full swing: what goes into crafting a story that's free of projection? How do you make it as simple as possible, but not any simpler? When you say that you're free of symbolism, how do you actually demonstrate that you are, if that's the aim, that is, to be free of symbolism? When you call your practice of reading cards 'intuitive' or based on literalism, or on what you see is the case, do you also start with identifying what is precisely *not* the case? What is your decisive factor in determining what is not the case? How many eyes do your read your cards with?

Reading List

CALVINO, Italo (1977). *The Castle of Crossed Destinies.* Vintage Books.

DECKER, Ronald, Depaulis, Thierry, Dummett, Michael, (1996). *A Wicked Pack of Cards: The Origins of the Occult Tarot.* St. Martin's Press.

ELIAS, Camelia, (2020). *Tarot Tracings: Essays in Literature and Divination. Italo Calvino, Robert Browning, W.B. Yeats, Rachel Pollack.* EyeCorner Press.

——— (2019). *What is Not: Marseille Tarot à la Carte.* EyeCorner Press.

——— (2019). *Divination with Cards: A Short History.* EyeCorner Press.

——— (2018). *21+1 Fortune-teller's Rules: Read like the Devil Manifestos.* Edited collection. EyeCorner Press.

——— (2015). *The Oracle Travels Light: Principles of Magic with Cards.* EyeCorner Press.

——— (2014). *Marseille Tarot: Towards the Art of Reading.* EyeCorner Press.

ENRIQUEZ, Enrique (2011). *Tarology.* EyeCorner Press.

ETTEILLA (pseudonym of Jean-Baptiste Alliette) (1785). *Manière de se récréer avec le jeu de cartes nomées Tarots. Paris: Lesclapart.*

FARLEY, Helen (2009). *A Cultural History of Tarot: From Entertainment to Esotericism.* I B Tauris & Co Ltd.

FLORNOY, Jean-Claude (2007). *Le pèlerinage des bateleurs.* Editions letarot.com.

GÉBELIN, Antoine Court de (1781). *Monde primitif, analysé et comparé avec le monde modern. Monographie imprimée chez l'auteur.*

GUÉNON, René (2004). *Symbols of Sacred Science.* Sophia Perennis.

HUSON, Paul (2004). *Mystical Origins of the Tarot: From Ancient Roots to Modern Usage.* Destiny Books.

Jackson, Dawn R. (2006). *The Wise and Subtle Arte of Reading Cards as examined by a Witch who practices said Arte* [http://www.hedgewytchery.com/] Defunct website.

Jodorowsky, Alejandro (2004). *The Way of Tarot.* Destiny Books.

Kaplan, Stuart (1978) *The Encyclopaedia of Tarot.* Vol 1–4. United States Games Systems.

Katz, Marcus (2011). *Tarosophy : Tarot to Engage Life, Not Escape it.* Salamander and Sons.

Levi, Eliphas (2001). *The Key to the Great Mysteries.* Red Wheel/Weiser.

Marteau, Paul (1949). *Le Tarot de Marseille.* Arts et Metiers Graphiques.

Papus (2008). *The Divinatory Tarot.* Aeon Books.

Silvestre, Colette (1987). *Les Tarots.* Editions Grancher.

Unger, Tchalaï (1985). *El Tarot.* Editiones Obelisco.

Waite, A.E. (1910). *The Pictorial Key to the Tarot.* William Rider & Son.

Truffault, Philippe. Dir. (2014) *Mysteries of the Marseille Tarot.* Documentary film for ARTE.

Warwick-Smith, Kate (2003). *The Tarot Court Cards: Archetypal Patterns of Relationship in the Minor Arcana.* Destiny Books.

Williams, Paul (2008). 'The Poetry of the Tarot de Marseille.' At *Tarot Authentique.* [http://www.tarot-authentique.com/] Last accessed: December 12, 2014.

www.ingramcontent.com/pod-product-compliance
Lightning Source LLC
LaVergne TN
LVHW051108180726
843512LV00011B/764